Front and back cover:
Osorkon II as Osiris, between Horus and Isis
The Louvre.

Pages 2/3:
Tomb of Sennedjem at Deir el-Medina
West Thebes, Upper Egypt.

Page 6 :
Giza: the Sphinx
Lower Egypt.

Page 11:
Priest at prayer from the Late Period
The Louvre

Page 112:
Pendant with the cartouche of Ramesses II
The Louvre

Page 129:
Breast-plate in the form of a vulture from the New Kingdom
The Louvre

ISBN: 2.907670.31.X.
Printed and bound in Italy

Photographic credits:

R. M. N.: 1, 11, 15, 16, 21, 22/23, 31, 33, 35, 36, 39, 43, 45, 46, 48, 49, 58/59, 61, 62, 65, 67, 68, 71, 73, 81, 112, 129, 136.

Pix/Erhardt: 2/3.
Pix/Friedrich: 74/75.
Pix/Revault: 102/103, 108/109.
Pix/T.P.S: 77.
Pix/V.C.L.: 78/79.
Slide/Armor: 100/101, 104/105.
Slide/Lade: 29.
Slide/Mollenhauer: 40/41.
Slide/Okapia: 6.
Hervé Champollion: 25, 26/27, 83, 84/85, 86/87, 88/89, 91, 94/95, 98/99, 106/107, 111.
Nguyen Thuc Diem: 51, 52, 55, 56/57, 97.

Text: A. Gros de Beler.
Contribution: F. Boutmy.

PHARAOHS

Aude Gros de Beler

Foreword
Aly Maher el Sayed

PHARAOHS

Aude Gros de Beler

Foreword
Aly Maher el Sayed

FOREWORD

The Pharaohs... Who has not dreamt at the mere mention of this word that embodies such mystery and magic ? Who has not held his breath at the sight of the golden mask of Tutankhamun ? Who does not know the names of Ramesses, Tuthmosis or Akhenaten... ?

The word "Pharaoh", that originally meant "the great house" or "the palace" of the Chief or the King, gradually came to represent all that is great, that is the greatest, in other words, the King himself. But in the collective consciousness, the title of the sacred sovereign eventually merged with the entire civilization that ancient Egypt has transmitted to us across the centuries.

In reality, the interest, the fascination, the passion of the world for the Pharaohs stems to a great extent from the fact that they are not only the ancestors of modern Egypt, but also the precursors of civilization and humanism and that they remain a reference in world history. They built, studied, imagined, discovered, invented, visualized, organized, lit the sacred fires of learning in an era when virtually the entire earth was still covered by a mantle of darkness. They overcame material constraints and grasped the spiritual dimensions thus enabling us to dream of eternity.

Across thousands of years, they have sent us a message wrought in the walls of temples and monuments and kept intact by the stones... a message of wisdom and harmony, spirituality and beauty.

This message from the past remains as true today as it was thousands of year ago and this splendid book will, I am sure, help to better understand its meaning. The centuries pass, but Egypt remains true to herself, proud of her past, proud of her Pharaohs, confident in her future. She who has done so much to enrich the culture of humanity continues to contribute to the cultural heritage of the world.

Aly MAHER EL SAYED
Egyptian Ambassador

CONTENTS

THE NILE, A FERTILE VALLEY

Three thousand years of History

"Egypt is a gift from the Nile." This slightly simplistic view expressed by **Herodotus** is contradicted by the more realistic one taken by modern Egyptologists, who are constantly finding new proof that the greatest victory of the pharaonic civilization was its fantastic success in exploiting to the utmost the resources of a river that was certainly an asset to the country, but whose shifting course and, above all, whose whims required it to be managed not only to perfection, but with constant vigilance and hard work. For almost three thousand five hundred years, generations of Egyptians have benefited from a situation that was initially favorable but which demanded a considerable amount of strenuous effort. Around this sacred and blessed river, a civilization of great originality grew up, whose astonishing stability and perfect continuity cannot fail to impress us.

This human experience, the longest on record, has for almost two centuries, inspired a lasting fascination and allowed both specialists and ordinary visitors to recapture the life, history, glory and misfortunes of a people forever immortalized by its vestiges still found in the Nile Valley.

The Nile

With its 4,136 miles, the Nile is one of the longest rivers in the world. We think of it as an Egyptian river but, in reality, it has already accomplished more than three quarters of its journey when it enters Egypt. Its entry is spectacular: six regularly spaced cataracts shatter the peace of its progress toward the North, where it divides into a multitude of small branches, all flowing into the Mediterranean and giving the Delta its very special configuration.

The banks of the Nile form a long oasis between two deserts: the eastern and the western deserts, renowned ever since high Antiquity for their stone quarries and mineral resources.

The sources of the Nile

For the ancient Egyptians there is no doubt: the Nile is part of the universe. It is born at the first cataract and disappears into the marshes of the Delta; beyond, there is nothing. The Greeks and the Romans took a more prudent view and admitted that they did not know where the Nile came from, but they thought that its source was located at the bottom of a valley yet to be discovered. This task was considered to be impossible, and the Latin expression *"quaere fontes Nili,"* "search for the sources of the Nile," was coined, meaning "to undertake an impossible enterprise." **Herodotus** concluded from his travels in Egypt, around 450 B.C., that *"the sources of the Nile are said to be at the bottom of the chasms and to gush forth between two mountains, one of which is called Crophi, the other Mophi."* Another scientist in the 2nd century B.C., **Claudius Ptolemy**, writes that it rises in the "Mountains of the Moon," but he gives no further details as to their exact location.

In reality, the Nile feeds from two parent branches, the White Nile and the Blue Nile, which merge at **Khartoum**, the capital of Sudan. The discovery of the source of the Blue Nile dates back to the 17th century, when a Portuguese priest, **Father Paez**, found **Lake Tana** during a stay in Ethiopia. A small river, called the "Little Abbai," enters the lake from the West and flows out through its southern tip under the name of "Great Abbai," but this river is, in fact, none other than the Blue Nile.

Map of Egypt

This map of Egypt dates back to 1767. It divides the country into three provinces: Lower Egypt (green), Heptanomes (yellow) and Upper Egypt (red). Although the boundaries of the provinces are still the same, one usually speaks of the North and the Delta as Lower Egypt and of the South as Middle and Upper Egypt. The map shows the Sinai as attached to Arabia Petraea (Rocky Arabia), the present Saudi Arabia, whereas today's frontiers make it an integral part of Egypt. Apart from some inaccuracies of scale and contour, this map differs from that of modern Egypt in two major aspects: it was drawn up before two great projects profoundly altered the geography of the region: the opening of the Suez canal, inaugurated in 1869, which links the Mediterranean to the Red Sea, and the Aswan Dam, completed in 1971, which created the huge Lake Nasser reservoir.

MEDITERRANEE
BOUCHES DU NIL
ALEXANDRIE
Paraetonium
Antiphra
Adyrmachides
Mt. Ogdamus
Mareotis
EGYPTE INFER.
Naucratis
Saïs
Sebennytus
Tanis
Peluse
Nitrie
Helio-polis
Heroopolis
MEMPHIS
Babylon
Arsinoe
Aphroditopolis
Clysma
HEPTANOMES
Petite Oasis
Oxyrynchus
Cynopolis
Hermopolis
Antinoe bâtie par l'Empr. Hadrien
Cusa
Hieracon
Lycopolis
Hypsele
Petite Apollinopolis
Antaeopolis
Crocodilopolis
Canal selon Hasius
Panopolis ou Chemmis
Ptolemais dans le Nome de Thinis
Abydus
Grande Oasis
Petit Diospolis
Coene
Coptos
Tentyra
Phoenicon
Memnonium
Petite Apollinopolis
THEBES ou Grande Diospolis
Hermonthis
Latopolis
EGYPTE SUPERIEURE
Elethya
Grand Apollinopolis
ou THEBAÏDE
Ombi
I. Elephantine
Petite Cataracte
Syene
Phylae
Talmis
Tacompsus
ETHIOPIE
Hyera Sycaminus
Pselcis
Grande Cataracte
Primmis
Mt. de la Pierre Basanite ou Baran
DESERTS
Mt. d'Albastre
Mt. de Porphyre
Golfe d'Heroopolis
Drepanum Prom
MER ROUGE
Aphrodite
Mios hormos ou Port de la Souris
Port Blanc
Mt. Aeas
Montagne d'Emeraude
Hydreum de Jupiter
Hydreum d'Apollon
Berenice
Hydreum Trogloditique
JERUSALEM
Ascalon
Azot
Hebron
Gaza
Raphia
Rhinocorura
Ostracine
PALESTINE
Arad
Elusa
IDUMEE
Petra
ARABIE PETREE
Elana ou Ailath
Aziongaber
Pharan
Golfe d'Elana
Mt. Oreb
M. Sinaï
Elim
C. Pharan
L'EGYPTE
A PARIS
Chez Crepy 1767
ECHELLES
Stades des Grecs dont 8. font un mil
300 600 1200
Lieues de France 20. au Degré
5 10 20 40

It is first in the 19th century that the question of the sources of the White Nile is again debated. This quest has given rise to any number of books, films and other documents by many contemporary authors. The English explorer **Speke** was certain that it originated in **Lake Victoria**, an enormous body of water covering 26,000 square miles the second largest lake in the world, straddling Uganda, Tanzania and Kenya. More precisely, he determined that **Rippon Falls**, just north of the lake, were the actual source of the White Nile. His opponents, the English adventurers **Baker** and **Burton**, were inclined to favor **Lake Albert** to the northwest of **Lake Victoria**, and **Lake Tanganyika** on the border between Burundi and Zaire.

Whom to believe? This is the mystery that the English journalist **Stanley** sets out to solve. After a quest lasting more than seven years, he discovers **Lake Victoria** at the headwaters of the White Nile: **Speke** was right. That is not all. West of **Lake Victoria** he finds the legendary "Mountains of the Moon" mentioned by **Claudius Ptolemy** and called Ruwenzori by the Africans. In memory of this important discovery, the mountains were renamed "Marguerite and Alexandra Peaks."

The flood of the Nile

The floods are caused by the heavy rains that fall in the Ethiopian mountains where the Blue Nile rises. The water, carrying a great load of silt scoured from the volcanic terrain, arrives in Egypt, where it fertilizes the land and feeds the crops. The flood leaves the Tropics at the end of May and does not arrive in Egypt until the end of June or beginning of July, which is why the Egyptians counted three seasons: **Akhet** (the flood, from June to October), **Peret** (sowing, from November to February) and **Chemu** (harvest, from March to June), the period of drought.

The pharaonic texts explain the flood with unyielding logic. In an underground cavern, close to the first cataract, three divinities reign, guarding the sources of the Nile: *Khnum*, *Satis* and *Anukis*. Every year they draw water from the reserves collected by *Ha'py* and release enough silt to nourish the crops. It therefore seems perfectly natural to dedicate a special cult to *Ha'py*, who is the personification of the flood and the symbol of the fertility of the river. He is, in fact, enormously popular and from North to South he is continuously given gifts and offerings and implored to grant the country a good flood.

The entire Egyptian political system is founded on this physical and geographical condition: strong political power is needed to safeguard the irrigation and insure the best possible distribution of the flood water by means of dams, dikes and irrigation channels. In short, water is ever the main preoccupation of the Egyptians, and evidence of this concern is manifold: on the royal lists, the year, the name of the king and the height of the Nile flood are mentioned in that order. Moreover, water is the typical offering to the deceased, who is threatened with being deprived of it if he ceases to grant requests addressed to him.

It is therefore of prime importance not to disturb the land covered by the flood. Towns and villages are built on desert land or out of reach of the flood. It is considered as a divine gift, all the more so, because the country is subjected to Saharan weather conditions with very little rainfall, scorching winds and large temperature variations. However, the arrival of the flood, its volume and duration are unpredictable: about half of the floods are considered too weak. This is why it is so important to manage it correctly, to obtain maximum benefit from it when it comes. The role of the authorities is therefore to maintain the whole system that controls the flood and, if there is a surplus of water, to store it for use in times of drought. This explains why there is famine in Egypt during periods of anarchy, when the country is politically divided and the dikes, dams and canals are no longer maintained and the land is lying fallow.

Dams on the Nile

Manage the flood, regulate the river, tame the violence of the cataract: these were said to be the primary motivations for the building of the Aswan Dam. To regulate the flow of the first cataract, the English had built the first dam, the **"Old Dam,"** in the 19th century. However, in 1955 the Egyptian government launched the idea of the **"High Dam,"** which would impound several floods and control the flow rate all the way to the Delta. The work on the dam started in 1960 as a result of an agreement between Egypt and the Soviet Union, and it was finished eleven years later, when President **Sadate** had succeeded President **Nasser**.

Limestone ostracon

When the material used to write or draw on is a shard of limestone or a piece of broken pottery, the document is called an ostracon. Generally, the texts consist of lists of things to remember, scribbles, informal messages, rough drafts, anecdotes, etc. Ostraca are our loose leaves, our "post-it." This ostracon from the New Kingdom transcribes Chapter 17 of "the Book of the Dead," which provides the deceased with the spells that he must recite to enter the underworld and to leave it when he chooses: "Here begin the hymns of adoration to be pronounced when, having come out into the Full Light of Day, the deceased may show himself at will in any form of life. Sitting in a hall, he can play checkers or he may, as a living soul, undertake great journeys. He must say..." *Then follow, written in carefully drawn columns, the sacred words to be recited by the deceased, in order to avail himself of this power.*

The sarcophagus of Nakhty

In an Egyptian funeral, the sarcophagus occupies a place of major importance. The texts explain how the deceased lives inside it as in the house he occupied on earth, how he can come and go at will through the door traced on the sides and how the two skillfully drawn eyes allow the deceased to observe the life of the living without having to move about. The wedjat eye, a combination of a human eye and that of a falcon, symbolizes the physical integrity without which no one can survive. During the Middle Kingdom, commoners are buried in painted wooden sarcophagi, some of which are beautifully crafted; for example, that of the chancellor Nakhty, who was in office during the 12th dynasty in the Asyut region.

The resulting reservoir, **Lake Nasser**, is no less than 300 miles long and 6 to 19 miles wide with a depth of almost 300 feet. The dam wall is 360 feet high, 3,200 feet thick at the base and 11,700 feet long, and can by its sheer weight withstand the pressure of the 5,500 million cubic feet of water in the lake. It is true that the Nile has been harnessed, since the last flood occurred in 1961, but after more than thirty years the impact of the dam leaves both Egyptian and foreign experts with serious doubts. One is forced to admit that the "concrete monster," that was to save the country from all its trials and speed it on its way to industrialization, has been a terrible economic, geographic and archeological disaster whose consequences increasingly threaten the country.

History unfolding

Documents of many different kinds help to further our knowledge of the ancient Egyptians: the Old Testament, the Hittite Archives, the Babylonian and Assyrian archives, Greek texts and, in Egypt itself, archeological remains and inscriptions (in the temples, funerary biographical notes, king lists, etc.) as well as literary works. However, in spite of these valuable documents, the actual history of Egypt is still almost a blank. There are hardly any, or very few, historical texts; we have names, dates, occasional events, isolated accounts. According to estimates, eleven dynasties out of the thirty that existed are sufficiently well known, but we know nothing, or very little, of the periods of transition or upheaval. A veil of darkness seems to cover nearly two thirds of Egyptian history.

Even the chronology presents a problem, despite the existence of extremely important documents. The annals of the **"Palermo Stone,"** incomplete and of unknown origin, tells of events that occurred between the reign of ***Narmer*** (the first pharaoh of the 1st dynasty) and that of ***Neferirkara*** (the third pharaoh of the 5th dynasty). The **"Room of the Ancestors"** shows ***Tuthmosis III*** making an offering before fifty-seven kings, thought to be his immediate predecessors. As to the numerous lists from the Ramesside era, drawn up by ***Sethos I*** and ***Ramesses II***, they contain all the names of the so called legitimate rulers from the beginning.

The most frequently used document remains the king list by **Manetho**. He was a priest from **Sebennytus** who lived in the 3rd century B.C., in the reign of the ***Ptolemies***. He divides the one hundred and ninety pharaohs into thirty dynasties, from the unification of Egypt by king ***Narmer*** to the conquest by ***Alexander***. Unfortunately, his work, the *Aegyptiaca*, is only known to us through late copies, as the original text was burned in the fire of the Great Library in **Alexandria**. Despite the importance of this historical source, the totally random character of his division into dynasties remains a mystery. In many cases, the kings of the same dynasty have no family links, unless these links are still unknown, and, conversely, the dynasty may change from father to son. Moreover, the dynasties are very unequal in nature: some are fictitious (the 7th dynasty includes seventy kings in seventy days), some are concurrent (the 22nd and the 23rd dynasties, for example), some number very few kings (***Amyrtaios*** is the only representative of the 28th dynasty), some have a great number (the 18th dynasty numbers fourteen kings and the Ramesside dynasty at least eleven pharaohs by the name of ***Ramesses***).

With these informations furnished by **Manetho**, Egyptologists have divided the thirty dynasties into **Kingdoms**, periods that were favorable and prosperous, and **Intermediate Periods**, of which almost nothing is known, corresponding to dark ages of economic, political and social turmoil.

The problems of dating

The exact dating of events is still today one of the archeologist's major headaches. At the beginning, it is quite usual to take as a starting point the cattle census that took place every two years: *"The year following the 10th census of all the oxen."* From the Middle Kingdom onward, most events are dated with reference to the first year of the king's reign: *"Year 4 of the reign of* ***Ramesses II****,"* for example. With the beginning of each new reign, the counting started again at Year 1. However, in times of trouble, it seems that no rules were observed, which makes it rather difficult to rely solely on this criterion to arrive at a precise dating. Furthermore, even in peace time, the real and effective duration of a reign is not always known. In this context, any dating criterion is apt to lead to imprecise conclusions.

Egyptologists have therefore established an Egyptian chronology based on fixed data determined by astronomical observations.

The ancient Egyptians used two calendars: the lunar calendar, reserved for religious feasts, and the solar calendar for secular events. The latter consists of twelve thirty-day months to which are added five extra days, dedicated to *Osiris*, *Isis*, *Horus*, *Seth* and *Nephthys*, i.e., three hundred and sixty-five days. Each thirty-day month is divided into three ten-day periods, each day lasting twenty-four hours. The Egyptians start their year on the first day of the flood. They soon discovered that the day when the flood started was marked by an astronomical phenomenon: on that day, the star **Sothis**, also called **Sirius**, appeared at the same time as the sun. This phenomenon is called the heliacal rising of **Sirius** and it was chosen as the starting point of the Egyptian year, which thenceforth began with a physical and an astronomical phenomenon, on July 19th.

However, the solar year has, in fact, three hundred and sixty-five days and a quarter. Consequently, the Egyptian year was twenty-four hours short every four years, and only after one thousand four hundred and sixty years, the so-called Sothiac period, did the three phenomena, the rising of the sun, the rising of **Sirius** and the start of the floods, again occur together on the first day of the Egyptian year. We know that this happened in 139 A. D.; therefore, we deduce that it did so in 1321, 2781 and 4241 B.C. In the course of time, the discrepancy increased until the summer feasts were celebrated in winter and vice versa. Scribes have carefully recorded, on several occasions, the time lag between the rising of **Sirius** and the beginning of the official year. With the help of these observations it has been possible to establish fixed dates that allow a more precise dating of the events mentioned in the documents.

Kingdoms and dynasties

The **Old Kingdom** (2780 to 2260 B.C.) follows a rather ill-defined period, the **Thinite Period**, during which Egypt is united under one single ruler and, in an almost definitive manner, lays down its religious, political and administrative rules and determines the form of its script and artistic canons.

This glorious kingdom constitutes the high point of classical Egypt. The kings adopt **Memphis** as their capital, whence the name Memphite Kingdom, used to describe it. In this era, the country achieves an exceptional degree of refinement. Stone architecture makes its first appearance. The kings choose to be buried in pyramids, whereas the commoners are entombed in **mastabas** where wall carvings and paintings depict, in minute detail, scenes of daily life. The 6th dynasty experiences a sharp decline in the royal authority, emphasized by the increased power of the provincial governors, whose office becomes hereditary and allows them to establish dynasties of their own with powers that sometimes exceed those of Pharaoh himself. Local civil servants become emancipated and Egypt seems threatened by foreign invaders. The king's authority, weakened by the long reign of ***Pepy II***, is incapable of redressing the situation, and Egypt plunges into a period of great turmoil: the **First Intermediate Period**. Total anarchy prevails: petty kings seize power, the nobility is deprived of all their possessions, the fields are deserted and famine haunts the country.

The reunification of Egypt under one single authority heralds the arrival of the **Middle Kingdom** (2040 to 1785 B.C.): in the Year 15 of his reign, **Mentuhotep I**, prince of **Thebes**, becomes the pharaoh of Upper and Lower Egypt. This new era of prosperity is marked by a number of political, administrative and religious reforms. Economic progress requires the opening up of new lands: the **Sinai**, the Libyan desert, the Arabian desert, **Nubia** and **el-Faiyum**.

Nevertheless, for reasons that remain obscure, the 12th dynasty ends in famine, internecine quarrels and foreign invasions. It does seem clear, however, that the arrival in Egypt of the **Hyksos**, no doubt from Asia, destabilizes the country, which then tumbles into another unsettled period: the **Second Intermediate Period**. The **Hyksos** reign sometimes in the North, sometimes over all of Egypt from their capital, **Avaris**, located in the western Delta. However, at the beginning of the 17th dynasty, the Theban princes mobilize to expel the invaders.

With the **New Kingdom** (1570 to 1085 B.C.) a new era of splendor and refinement dawns: the power of the kings is re-established, there is great territorial expansion and influx of riches from abroad. The pharaohs adopt as their capital **Thebes**, "the City of a Hundred Gates," which very soon becomes a symbol of prosperity, splendor and luxury. However, the increasingly important role of religion and the clergy in affairs of state inevitably leads to a deterioration of the royal authority. The Kingdom, undermined by waning authority and internal conflicts, corrupt and debilitated, can no longer withstand the pressure of foreign powers massing at the frontiers of Egypt.

The unrest of the **Third Intermediate Period** hastens the slow but inevitable decline. Outside threats combine with internecine struggles. An enfeebled central government can no longer resist the growing influence of the clergy of *Amun*, who seizes power in the South. During the 21st and 22nd dynasties, the Theban clergy rules over Upper Egypt while Pharaoh settles in **Tanis** and reigns in the North. The two succeeding dynasties are mainly occupied with repulsing the attacks of Nubian invaders. To no avail, however, as the 25th dynasty is Ethiopian: ***Piy***, king of **Napata** seizes power. After having defeated prince ***Tefnakht***, he gradually subdues the south of the country and his successor, ***Shabaqo***, installs his capital in **Thebes** and proceeds to conquer the Delta.

The **Late Period** (656 to 332 B.C.) is ushered in by a foreign invasion: **Assurbanipal**, an Assyrian king, arrives in Egypt and forces ***Tanutamani***, then in power, to flee to Sudan. ***Psamtek***, a prince of **Sais** (Delta of the Nile), assisted by the Assyrians, seizes the opportunity to conquer the country, thus creating the 26th dynasty. This dynasty is defeated by ***Cambyses***, who establishes the first Persian rule over Egypt: the 27th dynasty. Weary of Persian domination, the Egyptians organize uprisings all over the country. The only one to succeed is that of ***Amyrtaios***, in 405 B.C. He is the founder of the 28th dynasty of which he is the only representative because he is rapidly deposed by a prince from **Mendes** (Delta of the Nile), ***Nepherites I***, the first pharaoh of the 29th dynasty. The ensuing internal struggles cause ***Nectanebo I***, the founder of the 30th dynasty, to seize power. For a while, Egypt's past pharaonic glory is revived, but the Persian ***Artaxerxes III*** puts an end to this great renaissance by defeating ***Nectanebo II*** and creating the 31st dynasty.

The temple of Abu Simbel

The Scottish artist Roberts traveled in Egypt and Nubia in 1838/1839. Many of his drawings from this journey have been preserved and allow us to visualize what the pharaonic monuments looked like before modern looters, who are responsible for the present dearth on many sites, were unleashed on the Nile Valley. A comparison between these drawings and the monuments also reveals the inevitable degradation of the reliefs and paintings that decorated the walls of the tombs and temples. Here, Roberts has preserved for posterity the "holy of holies" of the temple of Ramesses II at Abu Simbel where we see, from right to left, Re'-Harakhty, Ramesses II as a god, Amun-Re' and Ptah. The temple is oriented in such a way that twice a year the sun reaches the inner sanctuary: on the 20th of February the first sunbeam touches the statue of Amun-Re', then that of Ramesses; whereas on the 20th of October, the sun shines first on the figure of the god Re'-Harakhty, then on that of Ramesses. The god Ptah, guardian of the land of shadows, always remains in the shade.

[David Roberts (1796/1864).]

Entrance of the Temple of Aboo-Simbel, Nubia
David Roberts. R.A.

Painting from aTheban stela

The Frenchman Prisse d'Avennes, a key figure in the burgeoning science of egyptology, arrives in Cairo in 1829 as a hydrographer but swiftly abandons his profession to devote himself entirely to archeology. For more than twenty years, he travels the length and breadth of the Nile Valley and collects a profusion of notes, plans, sketches, drawings and surveys, which he publishes as soon as he returns to France in his Art History according to the Egyptian monuments from the most ancient times until the Roman occupation. *This stela from the 20th dynasty was found in Thebes and shows the deceased, doubtless a priest because he wears the leopard, which skin is reserved for the clergymaking an offering of water to two gods. Osiris, sitting down, encased in a mummy-shaped cocoon, holds the divine or royal insignia: the crook and the flail. Isis stands behind him wearing the traditional dress of a goddess and a crown with a high chair: this hieroglyph represents her name.*
[Prisse d'Avennes (1807/1879).]

Alexander the Great goes to war against the Persian empire and swiftly conquers Anatolia, Syria and Phoenicia. In 333 B.C., he enters Egypt, where the Persian rule has stirred up widespread discontent. He is hailed as a liberator, particularly since his pilgrimage to the oracle of *Amun* at **Siwa** appears to everybody as a sign of respect for the native gods. Here, he consults the oracle, who recognizes in him the Master of the Universe and Son of the god. He proceeds to found **Alexandria** and appoint a governor to administer the country. At his death, in 323 B.C., his son ***Philip Arrhidaeus*** becomes pharaoh. He is succeeded by fourteen kings, all named ***Ptolemy***.

This dynasty is entirely Egyptian and it whole heartedly embraces local religious practices and pharaonic traditions: most of the temples still standing in the Nile Valley date from this prosperous and magnificent period, that of Greek Egypt. Enter the Romans. However, neither ***Caesar*** nor ***Marcus Antonius***, who seizes power after ***Caesar***'s assassination, in 44 B.C., chooses to annex Egypt outright. The great queen of Egypt at the time, ***Cleopatra***, enthralls them both, one after the other, to safeguard and above all, to retain her own power over a kingdom gravely threatened by the Roman presence.

The outcome is tragic: in 31 B.C., the battle of **Actium**, lost by ***Marcus Antonius***, is followed by the invasion of Egypt by ***Octavius***, ***Caesar***'s adopted son and legitimate heir. After ***Marcus Antonius***' suicide, ***Cleopatra*** delivers **Alexandria** into the hands of the new conqueror and, when her attempts to seduce him fail, she commits suicide as well. Egypt now becomes a Roman province, but its status is different from all the others: first, it is Rome's major granary, second, its position at the junction of three continents (Europe, Africa and Asia) makes it a political focal point. As opposed to other provinces, it is governed directly by the Emperor, represented by a prefect. For reasons of political opportunism, the Roman emperors do not hesitate to adopt the complete royal titulary, but, although the change of regime is both brutal and sudden, culturally as well as administratively, Egypt conserves its own identity. The cults of *Isis* and *Horus* become very popular: throughout the country; temples are dedicated to them. And their fame, albeit modified, spreads rapidly to Rome and across its empire.

After a long period of rejection, Christianity triumphs and thereby causes a final and definitive break with the ancient world. In 313 A.D., ***Constantine***, the first Roman emperor favorably disposed toward Christianity, institutes certain religious reforms. However, not until the reign of ***Theodosus*** and his edict of 391, is paganism definitely outlawed in the Empire. Following this decision, temples and places of worship are closed or transformed into churches. In 395, the country comes under the rule of the Eastern Roman Empire, but after a great deal of religious quarrels, the Christians of Egypt unite to form a national indigenous church: the Coptic Church. The term **"coptic"** also denotes the last stage of the old Egyptian language and the script by which it is transcribed. The temple of *Isis* at **Philae**, which had escaped Roman intervention because it was situated in the extreme South of the country, is finally closed by ***Justinian*** in 551. Thus, the last believers in Egyptian paganism disappear for ever and, with them, the last remaining individuals still able to use the hieroglyphic script.

Egypt: a success story

July 1798: **Bonaparte**'s navy lands in **Alexandria**. It is a complete surprise because the team accompanying him is rather special: almost thirty-eight thousand men, of which some contingents are soldiers; but, above all, there is a great number of scientists, engineers, artists, economists, botanists and writers. In fact, **Bonaparte**, apart from his colonial ambitions, which nobody can deny, hopes to transform this undisciplined Turkish province into a modern westward-looking state and reveal to the world the splendors of its prestigious past. Unfortunately, circumstances oblige him to give a more military turn to the campaign than he had planned, and after three years of fighting the Turkish forces, who are supported by the British government, the French army is obliged to leave Egyptian territory in 1801, after having signed the documents of surrender. No matter. An enormous amount of work has been accomplished: hundreds of drawings, sketches, memoranda, surveys and stories have been gathered together. Among those taking part, one in particular stands out: he is **Vivant Denon** who was both a scientist and a writer and became the founder of egyptology in France. Born in 1747, he owes his participation in the Egyptian campaign to Bonaparte's wife, **Josephine de Beauharnais**.

Lith. par Levié. Imp. par Hangard-Maugé. Prisse d'Avennes. Publié chez Arthus Bertrand, Libraire.

OFFRANDE À OSIRIS

STÈLE PEINTE SUR UN CERCUEIL DE MOMIE

Napoleon considers **Vivant Denon** to be too old, although he is only fifty, but once in Egypt he works incessantly. He is attached to the army unit of **Desaix** and, while assiduously pursuing the Mamelukes, he never stops exploring the monuments of pharaonic Egypt. He is so persistent that, when he returns to France, he is appointed Director General of Museums, and founds the **Napoleon Museum** which, is the **Louvre** of today. He publishes *Travels in Lower and Upper Egypt during the Campaigns of General Bonaparte*, whose amazing success marks the beginning of renewed interest in Egypt.

Later, between 1809 and 1822, comes the publication of the twenty volumes of *The Description of Egypt*, containing all the data collected during the Egyptian campaign. This work completes, develops and adds detail to **Denon**'s book. The joint effect of these two publications exceeds all expectations. Within a few days, Egypt comes into fashion; from all over Europe, people gather to admire its marvels. However, very quickly, the greed of the travelers ushers in a period of organized plundering, during which Egypt is deprived of a great number of its monuments. The task of acquiring the treasures is entrusted to the foreign consuls posted to Cairo. Traveling the length and breadth of the country, they amass splendid collections, bought at low prices or simply stolen, which they then offer for sale to western museums. The two collections sold by the infamous pair **Salt**, acting for Great Britain, and **Drovetti**, acting for France, make up the greater part of the Egyptian Antiquities department of the **Louvre Museum** in Paris.

Champollion: the "Rosetta Stone"

While some people shamelessly rob to supply museums and private collections, others, like **Jean-François Champollion**, eagerly seize this opportunity to make the monuments speak after their long and total silence. How to decode the hieroglyphic script remains a complete mystery. The young prodigy is only sixteen years old when he decides to devote himself to solving this fascinating enigma. He soon turns to the study of the Coptic language, which he believes to be a late form of hieroglyphic Egyptian. He spends fifteen years reading, consulting and comparing every possible type of Egyptian, Coptic and Greek document.

The battle of the Pyramids

Bonaparte, on July 1st, 1798, landed in the bay of Abu Qir, near the port of Alexandria, at the start of a campaign that was to be both cultural and military, the "Egyptian Campaign." At the time, Egypt was ruled by the Mameluke sultans and, when organizing his expedition, Bonaparte's intention was twofold: liberate the country from Turkish domination, certainly, but he also wanted to reveal to the world the wonders of pharaonic history. This is why he brought with him so many draftsmen, scientists, artists, historians and engineers, altogether around thirty-eight thousand men. This oil painting depicts the battle of the Pyramids in which Bonaparte defeated the Mamelukes, on July 21st 1798. Despite this victory, the French were obliged by the Anglo-Turkish forces to leave the country in 1801 after having capitulated.

[F.L.J. Watteau (1758/1823).]

Jean-François Champollion

An outstanding personality and an eminent linguist, Champollion, nicknamed "the Egyptian," chooses his career when he is still very young: at the age of eleven, he decides to devote himself to the mystery of the hieroglyphs and, above all, to solve it. He was born in Figac, in the Lot region of France, in 1790, and rapidly proves himself to be a tireless scholar with an insatiable desire for learning. He is interested in everything: Greek, Latin, Hebrew, and he is still only a child.

Encouraged by a tutor impressed with the exceptional qualities of his pupil, his parents put him in the secondary school in Grenoble, where he meets the prefect of the region, Fourier, who has participated in the Egyptian campaign. Fourier takes an interest in the boy and gives him a scholarship. Champollion becomes a boarder at his school and takes every available opportunity to further his knowledge of languages, adding to his other studies those of Arabic, Syriac, Aramenian, for the sole purpose of getting closer to Egypt... and the hieroglyphs.

At seventeen, having finished his schooling, he goes to Paris with the aim of learning Persian and Coptic -specially Coptic because he feels that this language is the only one that will help him unravel the mystery of the Egyptian script. Having finished his studies in Paris, he returns to Grenoble, obtains a Ph.D. and becomes professor of history. In his spare time, he still immerses himself in the documents from the Egyptian Campaign, examining all the copies of the incomprehensible hieroglyphic texts. Are they ideograms or phonograms? Or both? When some political problems force him to flee to Paris, Champollion obtains a copy of a most important document: the "Rosetta Stone." The inscription in three different languages -Greek, demotic and hieroglyphic- finally gives him the key to the mystery.

"I have got it!" On the 14th of September 1822, after more than twenty years of hard work, Champollion has finally cracked the hieroglyphic code. It is a combination of ideographic and phonetic writing. Subsequently, even after the official announcement of his discovery in the "Letter to Mr. Dacie," he continues his research and decides to go to Turin to examine the objects in the Drovetti collection. He comes back full of enthusiasm but with a nagging desire: he would like to go to Egypt to try out his recent discovery, to see if his system of interpreting the signs can be applied to any Egyptian text from any period.

In 1828, he finally fulfills his dream: he leaves for Egypt at the head of a Franco-Tuscan expedition including many experienced draftsmen. The journey lasts fifteen months during which he travels from Alexandria to Aswan visiting temples and tombs, copying inscriptions and engravings and decoding everything within sight. He observes that his alphabet "can be used with equal success for the Egyptian monuments from the Romana and Ptolemaic times and, what is even more interesting, for the inscriptions on all the temples, palaces and tombs of the pharaonic era." Completely worn out, he dies at forty-two years of age, leaving behind a considerable body of work.

He works incessantly, buried for days on end in libraries, pursuing every clue that might help further his research. In 1822, on the 14th of September to be more precise, his dream finally becomes reality: he understands how the hieroglyphic script works. To find out how he achieved this, one must go back to the year 1799. **François-Xavier Bouchard**, officer in the French army in Egypt, finds a great black basalt stela at **Rachid**, a city in the Delta, 70 kilometers from **Alexandria**, and carries it off to Cairo. This is the **"Rosetta Stone."**

The stone was taken from Cairo by the English, after the capitulation of the French two years later and is now to be found in the Egyptian collections of the **British Museum**. **Champollion** therefore has to work on copies of the inscriptions. The **"Rosetta Stone"** has an inscription in three different scripts that seem to repeat the same text: the top section is inscribed in hieroglyphs, the middle one in cursive demotic, (a late version of popular Egyptian), and the lower section is in Greek. The text is a decree by ***Ptolemy V Epiphanes***, promulgated in 196 B.C. in **Memphis**. Several scientists had already examined this extraordinary document, but in order not to be influenced in any way, **Champollion** decides to start afresh. He first notices that the royal names are enclosed in a cartouche and, second, that four hundred and eighty-six Greek words are needed to transcribe one thousand four hundred and nineteen hieroglyphic signs. This means that, to express an idea or a word or a concept, the Egyptian language uses not only ideograms but also phonetic signs.

He therefore starts by deciphering the names and eventually manages, through deductions and comparisons with the Coptic alphabet, to determine the real value of the signs. One year later, **Champollion**, at the age of thirty-three, is ready to publish his discovery: his *"Letter to Mr. Dacier"* sets out the general outline of how the Egyptian script works. Published in 1824, his *"Precis of the hieroglyphic system"* offers a more detailed and extensive explanation of his work and finally convinces the remaining skeptics.

Jean-François Champollion

This portrait, painted by Mrs. de Rumilly, shows Champollion transcribing on a sheet of paper an alphabet where the demotic and the hieroglyphic signs are shown side by side. Lost since the 6th century, when Justinian closed the temple of Philae, the pharaonic script came alive again only through the work of Jean-François Champollion. In 1822, after many years of hard and dedicated work, he succeededed in breaking the code of the hieroglyphs.

The hieroglyphs

In theory, every sign may:

• write the represented thing (ideogram): a boat for "boat," a bovine for "ox" or "cow";

• write, as a rebus, the corresponding consonants (phonogram); there is usually no notation for vowels;

• be at the end of the word and not pronounced, in which case it classifies the word in a category of menaning (determinatives).

For example, the sign (pr,) the plan of a house may mean: the word "house," the consonants p+r in another word (hpr, be born) or, placed at the end of the word, it may indicate that it concerns a building or part of a building.

Gradually, the signs become more specific.

• The uniconsonantal signs are alphabetic signs (twenty-four consonants or semi-consonants) which originally corresponded to word-signs of one single consonant, used as our alphabetic letters to note the various consonants:

d , n , r .

We do not know how ancient Egyptian was pronounced and even our knowledge of the consonants is very approximate. Our transcription (a kind of decoding of the hieroglyphs to make them easier to remember) is therefore partly a convention and excludes any possibillity of speaking this Egyptian language.

• The biconsonantal signs are those that have the value of two consonants: dd , ms .

• The triconsonantal signs are those that have the value of three consonants: nfr , ʿnh .

• The generic determinatives are signs that are not pronounced and, added to the end of a word, determine the category to which it belongs:

for things that have to do with scribes or writing ,

to denote abstract concepts ,

for things that have to do with hostile peoples

to determine death ,

for things that concern navigation

Concurrently, the notion of phonetic complements appears; they confirm one, or sometimes several, of the consonants, of a biliteral or triliteral sign. This results in: hpr, , "become, be born,"

hpr+p+r

or, using the consonants h + p + r 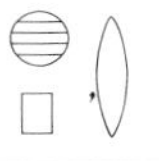

or even h + pr ,

or hpr + r where the last sign is the determinative of abstract words.

The number of possible ways to write a word are therefore, in theory, quite large. In practice, however, the possibilities are highly limited and only two or three possibilities are commonly used, although the others are not inaccurate: hpr or

Egyptian can be written from top to bottom, from right to left (this is the most common in Egyptian texts) or from left to right (which we use for simplicity since we are used to it). One never reads from bottom to top.

When the sign looks to the left, one reads from left to right: , dd, say. On the contrary, if it looks to the right, one reads from right to left.

The sentence construction is similar to ours except that the subject is placed after the verb: *"Gives Peter the book to the child"* instead of *"Peter gives the book to the child."* In certain cases the verb can be left out: *"Peter in the house"* instead of *"Peter is in the house."* Moreover, the article is often omitted: *"The book"* becomes *"Book."*

"Egyptomania"

Today, nobody knows exactly who deserves the praise, or the blame, **Bonaparte** or **Champollion**, for igniting the passion for the Nile Valley. Let us say that both of them contributed greatly, maybe in different ways: **Bonaparte** as the Father of the "egyptomaniacs" and **Champollion** as Father of the "egyptologists." Both groups share the same passion for Egypt in all shapes and forms.

For almost two centuries, Egypt of the pharaohs has haunted our daily lives in innumerable ways: architecture, decorative arts, furniture, ornaments, jewelry, high fashion, theater, opera, films, comics, advertising, etc. In fact, it is everywhere. In the 19th century, only the upper classes adopt these decorative designs from the Orient. The army is the first to engrave its weapons or decorate its banners with sphinx or lion-heads and extremely creative hieroglyphic signs.

The "Return from Egypt" style that was a direct result of **Bonaparte**'s Egyptian campaign, appears in the furniture of patrician houses in France. Stylish women of the time wear fabrics printed with hieroglyphic patterns and Egyptian-style jewelry. In 1922, the discovery by **Howard Carter** of the tomb of ***Tutankhamun*** gives the movement a great boost: the West, hungry for the Oriental experience, floods into **Valley of the Kings** and brings back all kinds of motifs inspired by pharaonic traditions which are then used on ornaments and fashion accessories.

The impact of the traveling exhibit **"Tutankhamun,"** shown in all major European capitals, is enormous. This is 1970: egyptomania hits all social groups. The fascination of ancient Egypt affects rich and poor, adults and children, art lovers or people who are simply overwhelmed. It marks the beginning of a string of exhibitions that attract thousands of visitors. In Paris there were: 1976, **"Ramesses the Great"**; 1987, **"Tanis, the Gold of the Pharaohs"**; 1993, **"Amenophis III, The Sun Pharaoh"**; 1998, **"Alexandria."** Who has not seen *The Ten Commandments* by Cecil B. De Mille or read *Death on the Nile* by Agatha Christie or *The Mysteries of the Great Pyramid* by Jacobs? Who has not dreamt of, one day, making the Journey to Egypt to walk in the footsteps of the glorious pharaohs?

Ramesses II conqueror of the Libyans

Ippolito Rossellini is the head of the Tuscan expedition that accompanies Champollion on his Egyptian journey in 1828 and 1829. Together they travel throughout Egypt from the city of Alexandria to the temple of Abu Simbel, producing a tremendous amount of documentation: they draw and paint reliefs and paintings, copy inscriptions, survey temples, etc. In The monuments of Egypt and Nubia, *Rossellini shows the results of fifteen months of work. This scene is from the columned hall of the temple at Abu Simbel. The victorious hero, Ramesses II, lunges at a Libyan whom he is about to run through with his spear, while a slain enemy lies prone under his feet.*
[Ippolito Rossellini (1800/1843).]

PHARAOH, GOD INCARNATE

The king: his role and attributes

"He is the one who multiplies property, who knows how to give. He is god, king of gods. He knows the one who knows him. He rewards the one who serves him. He protects his followers. He is Re' whose visible body is the disk and who lives for ever."

Without a doubt Pharaoh is an exceptional being: son of the gods and privileged intermediary between gods and humans, he is placed on the throne of Egypt to insure the observance of the *Ma'at*, i.e., justice, truth, order, trust and all the elements of stability that make the world inhabitable. There is no temple, shrine or chapel without a representation of Pharaoh in all his glory: whether he worships the gods or leads his armies,Pharaoh is the powerful master of all his surroundings. He rules over high and low, is endowed with invincible strength that overcomes everything, and he always acts according to his own will because, as the texts proclaim: *"all that he orders comes to pass."* His subjects love, worship and venerate him because Pharaoh knows how to guarantee their happiness, prosperity and protection. **Sinuhe** the Egyptian, favorite of ***Amenemhet I***, reports: *"While I was lying prostrate, I lost consciousness in front of Him."* His aura and his power are such that if he dies, the country is exposed to a terrible peril: that of returning to chaos. The accession of his successor recreates the order wanted by the gods, prescribed by the laws and desired by the humans.

His attributes remind everybody that he is a god among humans. Like the gods, he wears a false beard on his chin and, like *Osiris*, he holds in his hand the insignia of high rank: the scepter, **heka**, and the flail, also called **flagellum**. On his forehead, he has the eye of *Re'*, the **uraeus**, a cobra with raised head that crowns his headdress and is destined to protect the king at all times and to repel potential enemies. Pharaoh is never bareheaded: each one of his crowns has a specific function. However, the most common ones are the **nemes**, a cloth bound around the hair, its loose ends framing his face; the double crown, called **pschent**, a combination of the white crown of Upper Egypt and the red one of Lower Egypt; and the **khepresh**, the blue war crown with round spots. His dress is a simple, pleated loincloth held up by a belt engraved with a cartouche bearing his name.

The royal palaces

This exalted personage can live only in an exceptional place. Unfortunately, no undamaged palace is still standing, but what is left suggests an elegant and spacious architecture. Space was a necessity: besides containing living quarters for the king, his family and his court, the palace is his place of work, and houses offices and audience chambers where the general administration of Egypt is centralized.

Archeological explorations at **Thebes**, on the west bank of the Nile, have unearthed remnants of a mudbrick palace built by ***Amenhotep III*** at the end of his life, called the "House of Jubilation" in the texts. Reception halls, apartments of state, living quarters, temples, barge repositories, granaries as well as various types of workshops bear witness to the intense activity that must have gone on there. Paintings and engravings describe the elegance surrounding the king and his court. Wooden or ivory patens for cosmetics, vials for scent and all manner of flasks made of colored glass, small statuettes of servant girls or guardian deities, sundry toiletries tell us of the refined lifestyle favored by the pharaoh.

Pharaoh as Sphinx

Nobody knows which king is portrayed here because the sphinx is totally devoid of inscriptions. However, by the style alone it can be dated to the 18th dynasty and, judging by the shape of the face, it might be from the reign of Amenhotep II. It is probable that, at the time, it stood on one side of the temple of Ptah at Memphis. Today, it has fallen down and its only companions are a few scrawny palm trees. The sphinx portrays the terrifying side of the king: the Pharaoh who exterminates his enemies, routs the rebels. It is often placed at the entrance of a temple or in a necropolis. The role of the sphinx and, by extension that of the king, is to watch over the gods as well as over the dead.
[Spinx of Mit-Rahina, Memphis, Lower Egypt.]

Origin of the royal titulary

On his accession to the throne of Egypt, Pharaoh chooses a set of names, intended to describe him and distinguish him from his predecessors and successors. Initially, only the first name, the Horus name, is used for the king but, already during the first dynasties, this titulary is extended and finally becomes a full protocol of five names, regularly used from the Middle Kingdom onward.

Name 1 - *The Horus name*
It presents the king as the incarnation of the falcon-god Horus. This name panel depicts the niched façade and enclosure wall of a palace, the serekh, topped by a falcon wearing the pschent, a royal crown consisting of a combination of "the White" of Upper Egypt and "the Red" of Lower Egypt.

Name 2 - *The Nebti name*
This name can also be translated as *"He of the Two Ladies."* It places Pharaoh under the protection of the two tutelary goddesses of Egypt: *Nekhbet*, "The one from El-Kab," the vulture-goddess of Upper Egypt who resides at El-Kab; *Wadjit*, "The House of Wadjit," the cobra-goddess of Lower Egypt who resides at Buto.

Name 3 - *The Golden Horus name*
Introduced by a picture of *Horus* sitting on the sign for gold, nub, this name reaffirms the unchangeable, divine and sublime nature of the body of *Horus*, consequently of that of Pharaoh, who is the living incarnation of the god.

Name 4 - *The Throne name*
This name can also be translated as *"He of the Sedge and Bee,"* the sedge being the emblem of the North and the bee that of the South. This is, in fact, Pharaoh's first name, which he receives when he is enthroned. It affirms his sovereignty over the two kingdoms that make up the country: Upper and Lower Egypt.
This name is written inside a cartouche, resembling an elongated loop of rope closed by a knot symbolizing Pharaoh's universal sovereignty; it confirms his total power over the world.

Name 5 - The Birth name
This name is the name of Son of Re'. It is also inscribed within a cartouche and confirms that Pharaoh is the son of the sun-god and of direct solar origin. Several kings can have the same name of Son of Re'. Today we commonly use it for the pharaohs: *Khufu, Tutankhamun, Ramesses*, etc.

As an example, this is the titulary of *Ramesses II*. All the names can be translated, even the Birth name, which enables us to see how meaningful they are.

Name 1 "Powerful bull beloved by *Ma'at*"
Name 2 "Who protects Egypt and vanquishes foreign countries"
Name 3 "Rich in years, great in victories"
Name 4 "Rich in Re's truth, chosen by *Re*"
Name 5 "*Re'* has given him birth, beloved by *Amun*"

The banquet scenes with graceful, scantily clad female dancers and musicians, pictures of hunting and fishing in the marshes or representations of life along the river are among the masterpieces of Egyptian art. In these colorful decorations, carved in slightly raised relief, there is a prevailing atmosphere of calm, leisure, happiness and sensuality.

Pharaoh's daily life appears to have been, in all respects, a replica of that of the god, and to follow a complex ritual similar to the daily worship in the temple: rising of the king, clothing of the king, appearance of the king before a crowd of courtiers who prostrate themselves at the sight of the great man: *"they smell the earth, drag themselves along the ground and direct their prayers to this perfect God, praising his beauty."* Then, Pharaoh sets to work: in particular, he sees his vizier, who comes every morning to report on the affairs of state so that, in case of problems, the proper decisions can be taken. Apart from dealing with government matters, the pharaoh is often depicted on stelas and carvings taking part in lavish banquets enlivened by music and dancing.

Unfortunately, no matter how exceptional he is, the pharaoh remains human and subject to illness and, of course, old age. Therefore, to renew his strength and vigor, a ritual is performed, the **Heb-Sed**, intended to regenerate the physical and magical powers of the king. This is a ceremony where Pharaoh visits a number of sanctuaries in Upper and Lower Egypt and carries out certain rituals to recapture his strength and powers: archery and foot racing furnish proof of his rejuvenation. In principle, the **Heb-Sed** is celebrated after thirty years of office, but certain calculations show that, in reality, it was much more often, maybe every ten years, as some pharaohs refer to several jubilees during their reign.

Stories of conspiracies

In spite of all this love and attention devoted to Pharaoh, historical records tell of numerous conspiracies, intrigues and assassinations targeting the royal personage. Surprisingly enough, the most daring plots to overthrow the pharaoh were hatched in the harems by concubines or jealous secondary wives.

The most publicized of all these plots is the one toward the end of the reign of ***Ramesses III***, when an attempt was actually made on the life of the august individual. The magnitude of the conspiracy against the pharaoh, the number and status of the conspirators, some from the ranks of the princes, demonstrate the deplorable state of the Egyptian government at the time.

It was thought for a long time that ***Ramesses III*** had not survived the assassination attempt and that the ensuing trial was organized by his son ***Ramesses IV***, but three recently found papyri, quoting this incident, allow us to conclude that ***Ramesses III*** was doubtlessly saved by an informer who revealed the plot, and that he could therefore preside over the trial himself.

Tiy, a secondary wife of ***Ramesses III***, frustrated at seeing her son **Pentaur**, lose his chance to accede to the throne, decides to assassinate the old king in the hope that this desperate act will cause her son to be chosen as pharaoh, passing over all the other legitimate children. She obtains the cooperation of several palace officials, among them the great chamberlain in whom the king has total confidence. Altogether, thirty-two persons were directly implicated in the plot. It seems that the chances of success were thought to be considerable, since many high officials joined the plotters after having exhaustively discussed the terms with the harem women. As to the lower officials, they seem to have, at least, known about the conspiracy and some of them, who had been present at the meetings of the traitors, had preferred to keep silent. The guilty were hastily judged by a commission. The court minutes are short and stereotyped.

"The great criminal Pteuenteamun who was harem inspector. He was brought there because he had heard talk of the matters that the men had plotted with the harem women and he had remained silent. He was brought before the high officials of the Instructing Court. They judged his crimes, they found him guilty and they ordered him to be subjected to his punishment."

Only a few of the sentences pronounced by the court are known: cutting off the nose and ears for corrupt officials and death sentences for those of the guilty who were most seriously implicated. Apparently, persons of royal blood obtained the sinister privilege of putting an end to their existence by their own hands: it is thought that they were invited to commit "suicide."

Maspéro explains: *"... by examining a mummy found at Deir el-Bahri and known as "the mummy of the nameless prince." It is that of a male individual, twenty-five to thirty years of age, in good physical condition and without any injuries, who was buried without having been embalmed in the ordinary manner, the brain tissues had not been extracted, the internal organs were intact... Never has a face so clearly reflected the image of the most distressing and terrible death struggle. The horribly distorted features almost certainly indicate that the unfortunate man must have died of deliberate suffocation caused by his being buried alive."*

Pharaoh, head of government

The load of documents accumulating on the desks of the government authorities is enormous for the good reason that in Egypt, these authorities control everything in the name of Pharaoh, their undisputed head. Nothing escapes him. In the archives, we find documents of every conceivable type: office memoranda, lists of personnel, cadastral and fiscal surveys, wage dockets, various reports, complaints from the citizens, cautions and punishments by superiors, etc.

Senusret III

This extraordinary carving of Senusret III originates from Medamud in Upper Egypt where a quite original, because totally realistic, style developed during the Middle Kingdom. Despite the damaged state of this head, one can guess the sad expression of the king, who did not hesitate to let himself be represented, marked by age and exhaustion. The development of this style corresponds to a new awareness, born of the confusion during the First Intermediate Period: henceforth, Pharaoh is no longer considered as a god but as a man shouldering the burden of all too heavy responsibilities,

All this information, written down on papyri or **ostraca**, is presented in a competent and orderly manner: underlined, annotated, corrected in red ink, accounts in neat columns, and so on.

This administration, endeavoring to regulate all sectors of activity, is therefore extremely diversified and specialized: great teams of tenured officials, organized in intricate hierarchies, must know all about fields, cattle herds, granaries, building projects, ships, soldiers, frontiers, relations with foreign powers, commercial ventures, laws, prisons, health, etc. Apart from the royal administration, all provincial administrative units, all temples, all wealthy private individuals have their own bureaucracies. This gives an idea of the extent and complexity of the unwieldy state machinery. However, the pharaonic documents seem to suggest that throughout Egyptian history, the administration worked well when the country was in good order. When central government loses control over people and property, Egypt suffers every possible misfortune: invasion, war and, as ever, famine.

During the **Old Kingdom**, the system is bogged down by excessively centralized power where it is difficult to distinguish between what is a personal service to the "god-king" and what is service to the state. Centrally, the king chooses a vizier, who is the head of the executive branch and has absolute authority over all decisions. He is the director of four departments: the **Treasury**, which manages the economic sector and collects taxes; **Agriculture**, dealing with cattle farming and crops; the **Royal Archives**, where all title-deeds, civil acts, contracts, testaments, decrees, minutes, judgments and various law texts are carefully preserved; **Justice**, which is responsible for enforcing the law.

Locally, Egypt is divided into forty-two **nomes**, or provinces, administered by **"nomarchs"** commonly known as "canal diggers." They manage the economic activities in the region, maintain the irrigation system and supervise state land. During the Old Kingdom, the problems arise from the fact that these positions became hereditary. The state land becomes the basis for feudal regimes and the regional governors strive to seize the prerogatives attached to royal land. From the 4th to the decline of the 6th dynasty, local governors become very prosperous and gradually achieve independence.

In an attempt to redress the situation, the pharaohs create a number of new offices with direct links to the central government. However, these new charges remain totally illusory and symbolic: they include *"Head of the secrets that only one man sees," "Head of the secrets that only one man hears," "Head of the secrets of heavely mysteries," "The Only Friend," "The Carrier of Sandals," "The Caretaker of Crowns,"* etc. Thus, this extremely confused period of the declining years of the Old Kingdom is marked by a deterioration of central government, exacerbated by the rising power of local individuals and an external situation that becomes more threatening as the royal power declines.

The two most important areas of activity are, on the one hand, agriculture, and on the other, the great construction projects associated with royal funerary monuments and temples. These require large quantities of materials: quarried stone and precious or semiprecious stones. Pharaoh organizes huge expeditions to explore and mine the quarries and mineral resources in neighboring countries. He reserves the right to commandeer the rural population to work on his enormous building sites. The workers are generally paid in kind: clothes, food and shelter.

From the 1st dynasty, two occupations flourish: those of craftsmen and scribes. They are strictly controlled but confer considerable advantages. These men are greatly respected because they are representatives of the royal authority. Their corporations have a strict hierarchical structure which everyone must respect. The fact that, in **Giza**, **Saqqara** or **Maidum**, their tombs are always situated close to the great royal pyramid demonstrates their importance in Egyptian society.

During the **First Intermediate Period** the prestige of the pharaoh suffers a considerable downturn because these long years of unrest, exacerbated by severe drought, inspire certain doubts concerning the king's powers. The **"Lamentations of Ipuwer,"** which is the only text known from this very dark period, describe the inability of the pharaoh's government to manage this serious crisis.

"The Private Council of the king, now, its archives have been carried off and the secrets that they contained have been made public. The religious spells have been revealed. The offices have been broken open and their contents taken away. The scribes have been murdered,

Royal profile

It is very difficult to know whom the artists wanted to portray in this sketch. One thing is certain: it is a pharaoh because on his forehead he wears the royal uraeus, the cobra symbolizing the eye of Re' whose role it is to exterminate the king's enemies. The style of the features suggests that this work is from the 18th or 19th dynasty: maybe Tuthmosis III because of his slightly aquiline nose? Whoever it is, his profile is superb, although it is only a sketch, rapidly drawn on an ostracon.

their writings pillaged. The cadastral registers of the scribes are destroyed and the wheat of Egypt has become common property. The laws are spurned, they are trampled underfoot in public places and the poor break them in the street. Events have occurred that have never happened before: the king has been deposed by the common people. The one who was buried like a falcon is now deprived of offerings and what his pyramid hid is gone. The poor now own riches and the former owner has nothing left. The one who had nothing has a granary and his larders overflow with another's reserves. Nothing is in its place: it is like a flock moving at random, without a shepherd..."

Now, a great volume of pessimistic literature appears as a result of the economic and social distress. The **"Dialogue of the Desperate man with his soul,"** undisputed masterpiece of Egyptian literature, is simply the disillusioned statement of a man faced with a life where violence and incomprehension prevail.

"To whom can one speak today? Friends are wicked and brothers of today do not know how to love!

To whom can one speak today? Hearts are greedy and everyone tries to seize his neighbor's property; peaceful men fade away and the strong crush everybody!

To whom can one speak today? It is the triumph of Evil, and Good is cast down everywhere.

Amenhotep II

This fragment of a red quartzite head of Amenhotep II, a pharaoh of the 18th dynasty, is remarkable for the extreme purity of its lines and the almost life-like expression of the king: the hint of a smile lights up his stone face whose eyes seem to look straight ahead. The pharaoh wears the nemes, a striped cloth over his hair and across his forehead, crowned by the raised cobra, the uraeus, whose head has been broken off. His false beard is lost but one can clearly see, in front of the ears, the marks of the fasteners that held it in place.

Death is in my eyes as the cure is to the ill, like going out after having suffered.

Death is in my eyes as the scent of the lotus, like sitting down on the banks of the land of euphoria.

Death is in my eyes like a man's desire to see his house again after long years of captivity."

The **Middle Kingdom** thus re-establishes the pharaoh's power for a time, but henceforth the prestige of the king rests on his real power. Pharaoh moves closer to his people and relinquishes his position as ideal king, living incarnation of the gods, and becomes simply the head of the government and the army. A new, less centralized bureaucracy emanating from the provincial governments of the **First Intermediate Period** is put in place. Egypt reasserts its sovereignty over the neighboring territories to the West and the East, in particular over the **Sinai** because of its rich turquoise and other semiprecious-stone quarries, launches an active colonization of **Nubia** and develops the agricultural and economic management of **el-Faiyum** oasis, which had been ignored until then.

The painful experience of the **First Intermediate Period** and a logical analysis of all that happened in this period lead the king to take a more serene view of his office. As a precaution, Pharaoh associates his eldest son with the throne and teaches him, from an early age, the rules governing the arduous task of being king.

The **"Instructions of Amenemhet I"** to his son ***Senusret I***, a list of bitter observations, warnings and advice concerning the principles of government, date from this time:

"Keep your distance to your subordinates who are as nothing and whose intentions one does not heed! Do not mingle with them when you are alone, have confidence in no brother, know no friend. Never have a hanger-on: it serves no purpose. When you are resting, do the watching yourself because one has no friend when the evil day comes! I have given to the poor and educated the orphan, I have elevated the one who had nothing as well as the one who was prosperous, and he who ate my food now conspires against me! The one to whom I reached out my hand, now seizes the opportunity to stir up trouble! Those who wear my fine linen, now consider me as a doormat! Those who my myrrh anoints, now spit on me! The living images given to me -the humans- have fomented an unheard of plot against me and a great battle such as one has never seen!"

Still, in spite of his unfailing vigilance, **Amenemhet I**, powerless to quell the waves of violence and assassination attempts, dies in the Year 29 of his reign, when he falls victim to a plot apparently concocted inside the palace.

The beginning of the **New Kingdom** coincides with a radical change in Egyptian society which, from now on, has three centers of power: Pharaoh and the government, the clergy and the army. The king becomes a war hero, the incarnation of a war-god and a sun-god: *Amun-Re'*. He is the glorious and conquering hero, the universal sovereign, endowed with divine and superhuman qualities, son of the gods and privileged intermediary between them and the humans. At the head of the government is the king, aided by his viziers, called the **tjaty**, who are themselves assisted by the "Mayors of large cities," governors of well-defined territories who regularly send reports to their hierarchical superiors.

The region of **Thebes** becomes the administrative and religious center of the whole country. Why **Thebes**? The reason for this choice is twofold: to emphasize the power of the Theban Kingdom and move closer to **Nubia**. After the upheavals of the **Second Intermediate Period**, it is the Theban princes who go to war against the **Hyksos** invaders and undertake to reunite the country with their native city as its center of power. At the same time, the political and geographical situation begins to change. Egypt now extends into **Nubia** as far as the city of **Napata**, near the fourth cataract. It therefore seems quite natural to site the capital as close as possible to the center of the country. Moreover, it draws on its African kingdom for a considerable portion of its resources of gold, silver, precious materials, hides, ivory, incense, wood, quarried stone, manpower, etc. Thus, moving closer to **Nubia** becomes an overwhelming necessity.

Pharaoh, son and servant of the gods

One of the oldest tales, that we owe to the **Papyrus Westcar**, describes how **Redjedjet**, the wife of **Rauser**, Grand Priest of *Re'*, gave birth to the first three kings of the 5th dynasty. To help with this extraordinary birth, the goddesses *Isis*, *Nephthys*, *Meskhenet* and *Heqet* were called upon, as well as *Khnum*, the god who, according to certain traditions, was responsible for modeling humans on his potter's wheel.

"Then Isis stood in front of her, Nephthys behind her and Heqet quickened the birth. And Isis said: "Do not be forceful in her womb, in this your name of ***Userkaf****." Then this child slid into her hands: it was a child of one cubit's length whose bones were sturdy. His limbs were encrusted with gold and he wore a crown of real lapis lazuli. They washed him after his umbilical cord had been cut and he had been put in a brick frame. Then Meskhenet approached him and said: "A king who will wield power in the entire country," while Khnum gave health to his body."*

In fact, Pharaoh is in essence the carnal son of the god. This idea, although it is generally accepted, comes to the fore more frequently when there is a need to legitimize somebody's accession to the throne. Thus, in the 18th dynasty, queen ***Hatshepsut***, challenged by followers of ***Tuthmosis III***, decides to represent her divine filiation on the walls of her funerary temple at **Deir-el-Bahri**. The scene shows how the god *Amun*, in the form of ***Tuthmosis I***, unites with queen ***Ahmes*** to conceive the baby ***Hatshepsut***. In the background we see the potter-god *Khnum* and his associate, *Heqet*, as well as the group of the seven *Hathor*. After the birth, the gods present the divine infant to her father, *Amun*, and give her into the care of the great nurturing goddess, the cow *Hathor*, who will suckle her and watch over her.

An identical picture exists in **Luxor**, in the **"Chamber of the Birth of Amenhotep III."** These scenes are more detailed and minutely describe the different stages of the marriage with the god: the conception, the pregnancy and the birth. Here we have a more extensive set of gods: *Amun*, *Khnum* and *Hathor* but also *Isis*, assisting *Khnum*, *Thoth* who carries the message to the queen that she will give birth to a son destined to be king, *Taweret* and *Bes*, who preside over the birth and insure that all goes well, and the spirits of Upper and Lower Egypt as attentive spectators of the event and protectors of the divine infant.

The generalization of this concept, whose purpose is to endow the pharaoh with a divine filiation, dates only from the Late Period. At this time, the sanctuaries acquire a small additional building: the **"mammisi,"** translated as the "place of birth." Here, the mystery of the god-son is celebrated every year: *Khons* in the Theban triad, *Nefertem* in the Memphite triad and *Anukis* in the triad of **Elephantine**. By extension the god-son becomes the infant king: the pictures inside the sanctuaries describe, as for ***Hatshepsut*** and ***Amenhotep III***, the various episodes of the divine conception of Pharaoh.

As Pharaoh now enjoys such an intimate relationship with the gods, the laws regulating the practices at places of worship become more explicit. Because he is the son of the gods and their representative on earth, Pharaoh alone is allowed to approach them. His mission is to uphold the order of the universe and, in this capacity, he is the only person empowered to officiate in the temples. This causes a material problem: in view of the great number of sanctuaries crowding the Nile Valley; Pharaoh is incapable of carrying out this duty every day. Therefore, by royal deputation, the clergy assume the tasks of the daily observance of the divine rituals, even if, on the walls of the temples, only Pharaoh is depicted in this role. To avoid incurring the anger of the gods, who would not hesitate to order a definitive return to chaos, the king must build temples and shrines throughout the country and maintain them by continual offerings. In exchange, the gods grant him protection and assistance in all circumstances.

Pharaoh, supreme commander

In addition to his functions as head of state and religion, Pharaoh also has the title of Supreme Commander of the Armies. This office becomes all the more important when, from the New Kingdom onward, Egypt embarks on a program of territorial conquest: in **Libya** to the West, in **Nubia** to the South and in **Syria-Palestine** to the East. Pharaoh takes on the role of hero and warrior-king: he is *"as strong as Montu when he advances,"* according to the narrator of the battle of **Kadesh**. As underlined by the second name of ***Ramesses II***, his **Nebti name**, he *"protects Egypt and vanquishes foreign countries."* Here we have the military and imperialist program launched by these dynasties.

Texts and carvings illustrate this new policy. Striking power becomes one of the main qualities of Pharaoh: he is the one who *"enters into battle and never retreats, the Supreme General of his army, the brave warrior on his chariot, who grasps his bow and shoots to the right without missing his target, he who is on foot, powerful by his courage, his strong arm carrying the club and the shield, he who tramples kings under his sandals...."*

Amenhotep III

This royal head features Amenhotep III wearing the khepresh, the war crown, over which is coiled an uraeus, difficult to discern because its upper part is broken. Despite the hardness of the stone, granodiorite, the artist has succeeded in giving the face a very realistic expression enhanced by the hint of a smile that enlivens the soft, regular features of the king. In the 18th dynasty, this kind of work, typical of the reigns of Amenhotep III and IV, is a great innovation contrasting with the more formal and stereotyped art practiced during the preceding dynasties.

Amenhotep IV

Several of these statues of Amenhotep IV still exist. They come from the temple of Aten that the king built for himself at Karnak before deciding to reside in Tell el-Amarna. All the statues bear the name of Amenhotep, who later changed his name to Akhenaten. They show Pharaoh dressed in a simple royal loincloth, arms crossed over his chest, holding the heka crook and the flail. This statue was given to the Louvre Museum by the Egyptian government in recognition of French cooperation in the reconstruction of the Nubian temples.

Following pages

The temple of Ramesses II at Abu Simbel

The great temple at Abu Simbel is one of the most spectacular monuments ever built in Egypt. It is a rock temple situated in Lower Nubia, some 170 miles south of Aswan, and cut deep into the Libyan cliff face. It is the work of Ramesses IIand was dedicated to the sun-god Re'-Harakhty, to Amun and to the god-king. The three colossal statues decorating the front are 65 feet high and show the king sitting with his hands on his knees, his head covered by the nemes crowned by the pschent, the crown of Upper and Lower Egypt and the royal cobra, the uraeus. When the Aswan dam project was planned, the Egyptian authorities were forced to contemplate moving the temple, since it was threatened by submersion in the water of Lake Nasser. The international community was mobilized to save it. Today the temple is oriented as it was originally but... 260 feet higher up.

[Temple of Ramesses II, Abu Simbel, Nubia.]

From the 18th dynasty on, the walls of temples and funerary monuments are filled with scenes that depict royal conquests and illustrate the invincible strength of the sovereign. Pharaoh, who is shown in heroic proportions, i.e., gigantic, dispatches a handful of enemies with an ax while clutching them by their hair. This is a symbol of the victory of order over chaos, of the unquestionable supremacy of Egypt over foreign countries. Similarly, detailed accounts of battles become a common iconographic subject. The king in all his glory, followed by a handful of foot soldiers, hardly visible because they are so small, dominates the battlefield covered with dismembered corpses and enemies appealing for mercy. Then comes the inevitable scene of a victorious Pharaoh presenting *Amun* with an interminable line of fettered prisoners. At his feet, he has the "fortress cartouches," a kind of crenellated oval containing the names of the vanquished peoples, which he crushes under his sandals.

Some gods join the war effort: *Amun*, the dynastic god; Re' the sun-god; *Ptah*, the creator of **Memphis**; *Seth*, the ruler of thunderstorms; as well as *Montu*, who personifies irresistible strength in combat; the lioness-goddess *Sakhmet*, "The Powerful One," etc. The king identifies with the gods and never fails to give them numerous donations, gifts and offerings before a battle in order to be blessed with power and courage throughout the hostilities. On his return, as a token of thanksgiving, he offers a large portion of the booty to the clergy, who become extremely rich and acquire enormous economic assets. This is the case of the great temple of *Amun* at **Karnak** whose power and prosperity rapidly become a very real threat to the central government.

One of the most popular tales is that of ***Ramesses II***, pharaoh of Egypt, confronting **Muwatalli**, king of the Hittites. The event is the battle of **Kadesh**, immortalized as the **"Poem of the Pentaur"** and told to us by carvings on the temple façades in the kingdom. A subtle combination of text and drawings recounts this feat, a symbol of Egyptian victories over foreign powers as well as proof of the importance of royal propaganda during the Ramesside era.

"His Majesty started marching toward the North with his infantry and his chariots and after having departed without hindrance on the 9th day of the 2nd month of the summer in the 5th Year, His Majesty passed the fortress of Sile, as strong as Montu when he advances. All countries trembled before him and their rulers brought their tributes: all the rebels bow down for fear of His Majesty's authority."

The Egyptians arrive in the vicinity of **Kadesh** on the Orontes, where the two armies clash with each other.

"Thus, the vile Hittite had come there after having united in federation with himself all the countries as far as the sea (...). They covered the hills and the valleys like a swarm of locusts. He had saved none of his country's money and had stripped himself of all his property to give it to these countries so that they would go to war with him."

The Hittites, lying in ambush behind **Kadesh**, let the first Egyptian division pass, that of *Amun*, led by ***Ramesses II***, and attacked the division of *Re'*, which, taken by surprise, flees. ***Ramesses II*** then finds himself cut off from his armies and surrounded by the Hittites.

"His Majesty was informed of the event. His Majesty burst forth like His Father Montu. He gathered up his combat weapons, donned His chain-armor: it was Baal in action! (...) His Majesty spurred his horse and rushed at the vile Hittite, all Alone, with nobody accompanying Him! His Majesty advanced to look around him and saw Himself surrounded by two thousand five hundred chariots that closed in on Him and by all the scouts of the vile Hittite and of the numerous peoples that accompanied him."

Abandoned by his men, the king turns to Amun, who miraculously answers him. Fortified by the presence of the god, the king single-handedly cuts the enemy to pieces. The very next day, **Muwatalli** sends envoys to sue for peace in these terms:

"Your humble servant proclaims that you are the son of Re', physically descended from him and to whom he has entrusted all the countries together. As far as the country of Egypt and the country of the Hittites are concerned, they are your servants; they lie at your feet: it is your father, the divine Re', who has given them to you. Do not wield your power over us! Yes, your authority is great and your strength weighs heavily on the Hittite country. But is it good that you slay your servants, turning a terrible face toward them? Look: yesterday you spent your day killing one hundred thousand men and today you have come back and do not spare your heirs. Do not push your advantage too far, victorious king! Peace is better than war!"

However, if the Hittite archives are to be believed, it appears that ***Ramesses II*** retreated after a questionable victory where he succeeded only in saving his army from total disaster. The two warring armies left the battlefield without either of them having been defeated.

The great royal figures of the New Kingdom 1539 to 1080 B.C.

18th dynasty	1539 to 1514	*Ahmose and Ahmes-Nefertari*	*19th dynasty*	1293 to 1291	*Ramesses I and Satre*
	1514 to 1493	*Amenhotep I*		1291 to 1279	*Sety I and Tuya*
	1493 to 1481	*Tuthmosis I and Ahmes*		1279 to 1212	*Ramesses II and Nefertari*
	1481 to 1478	*Tuthmosis II and Hatshepsut*		1212 to 1202	*Merneptah and Isisnefret*
	1478 to 1456	*Hatshepsut*		1202 to 1199	*Amenemesse and Baketurel*
	1478 to 1426	*Tuthmosis III and Merytre Hatshepsut*		1199 to 1193	*Sety II and Tauosret*
	1426 to 1401	*Amenhotep II and Tiaa*		1193 to 1187	*Siptah-Merenptah*
	1401 to 1391	*Tuthmosis IV and Mutemuia*		1187 to 1185	*Tauosret*
	1391 to 1353	*Amenhotep III and Tiy*			
	1353 to 1336	*Akhenaten and Nefertiti*	*20th dynasty*	1185 to 1182	*Sethnakht et Tiy-Merenaset*
	1336 to 1335	*Smenekhkara and Merytaten*		1182 to 1151	*Ramesses III and Isis*
	1335 to 1326	*Tutankhamun and Ankhesenamun*		1151 to 1145	*Ramesses IV and Tentopet*
	1326 to 1323	*Ay and Tiy II*		1145 to 1141	*Ramesses V and Nubkhesed*
	1323 to 1293	*Horemheb and Mutnedjmet*		1141 to 1080	*Ramesses VI to Ramesses XI*

Princess from Tell el-Amarna

Excavations at Tell el-Amarna have unearthed fragments of a number of exceptional statues, some of which were found in the ruins of workshops of artisans and artists who worked mostly for the court and the royal family. These discoveries have shown that women had a very high standing among the royalty during the reign of Akhenaten. No queen is more famous than Nefertiti, and the princesses from Amarna are, doubtless, among the best-known of all the royal children in Egyptian history. This bust of painted limestone is part of the splendid portrait gallery and represents one of Akhenaten's daughters, wearing a striped bowl-shaped wig to which is attached a delicately worked braid.

Queens of Egypt

Whether they perform the role of King, are the "Mother of the King," "Great Wife of the King" or "Secondary Wife of the King," all, without exception, are given the same title: that of "Queen of Egypt." From the first dynasties onward, they enjoy definite privileges that set them apart from ordinary Egyptian women: statues, titles, tombs, etc. Initially, they have a pyramid, smaller in size, close to the royal tomb. Later, they are buried at a site, near the **Valley of the Kings** but distinct from the **Valley of the Nobles**: the **Valley of the Queens**. They wear the **ureaus** on their foreheads and, on their heads, crowns borrowed from the goddesses *Hathor* or *Nekhbet*. Their names are inscribed in a cartouche like those of the kings. Their titularies prove that they are of divine essence, associated with the crown, queens of the dual country, mistresses of the universe. They generally act as priestesses: their attributes are the sistrum of the goddess *Hathor* and the necklace **menat**, which they shake before the gods. Furthermore, they have a representational role at the pharaoh's side: they are often seen together with their son, father or husband as guarantors of the cosmic order.

However, in spite of their high standing among the Egyptian royalty, the queens seem to have been excluded from power, although, officially, any woman could perform the duties of the king. If, by chance, one of them succeeded in attaining this high office, it was more by accident or coincidence than by the will of the pharaonic regime. Their situation changes at the beginning of the New Kingdom: queens and princesses consolidate their power. Henceforth, they participate more actively in the political life of the country and sometimes become important figures in the royal government. At the beginning of the 18th dynasty, queen ***Ahhotep*** and, especially, the Great ***Ahmes-Nefertari***, respectively mother and wife of ***Ahmose***, are efficient and intelligent regents for ***Amenhotep I***, after the death of his father while he is too young to reign. In the course of time, the idea of a woman who is both queen of Egypt and a skilled politician becomes a generally accepted fact. There are many examples of close cooperation between royal husbands and wives. Whether it is queen ***Tiy***, included in all the scenes depicting her royal husband ***Amenhotep III***, or ***Nefertiti***, the beautiful, faithful wife of the heretic pharaoh ***Amenhotep IV-Akhenaten***, or ***Nefertari***, the Great Royal Wife of ***Ramesses II***, they are all well known for their personal contributions beside their husbands and their dynamic influence at the heart of the affairs of state.

However, in order for a woman to aspire to the throne of Egypt, being queen is not enough. This is proven by history: apart from the Greek queens, the various ***Arsinoes*** and ***Cleopatras***, we know of only six reigning women in thirty centuries. The few documented cases are similar and the result of a combination of various events. They all concern royal princesses who have become the wives of pharaohs. Often, the lack of an heir makes them regents in the period between the death of the king and the accession of his direct successor; a regency which evolves into kingship.

The manner in which ***Hatshepsut*** accedes to power is a perfect example: it is the result of a serious crisis caused by the lack of a male heir. ***Amenhotep I*** had only one son, **Amenemhet**, who died in infancy. Therefore, a descendant of a parallel branch, ***Tuthmosis I***, becomes the successor. As he wants to legitimize his power, he marries ***Ahmes***, one of the sisters of ***Amenhotep I***. This marriage produces two children: a son, **Amenemes**, who dies in childhood, and a daughter, ***Hatshepsut***. As in the previous case, the successor is again an illegitimate child: ***Tuthmosis II***, son of ***Tuthmosis I*** and a mere concubine, **Mutnefret**. To legitimize his claim to the throne, he marries his half-sister ***Hatshepsut***. However, he dies at the age of twenty-five, in Year 3 of his reign and, moreover, his only royal children are two daughters. Logically, ***Tuthmosis III***, son of ***Tuthmosis II*** and a concubine, **Isis**, should succeed him, but at his father's death, he is much too young to reign, so his stepmother, ***Hatshepsut***, becomes regent. Already in Year 2 of her regency, she has herself crowned king and, to legitimize her position, she declares that she is the daughter of the god *Amun* himself and queen ***Ahmes***. *"Because she understood the desire of the Egyptians to be governed by a man, she had herself represented as King."* She adopts the essentially masculine, royal attributes, such as the false beard, the loincloth and the crowns of Upper and Lower Egypt, and keeps the entire pharaonic titulary: she is ***Hatshepsut***, "Powerful bull loved in **Thebes**."

She reigns for twenty-two years and her successor is officially enthroned only after her death. We know very little about this somewhat unusual reign. For a long time, historians and egyptologists believed that ***Tuthmosis III*** had been excluded from the government of the country. Today, however, in the light of certain documents, many question this assumption: it seems rather to be a case of double authority, with queen ***Hatshepsut*** taking care of commercial and administrative matters, and pharaoh ***Tuthmosis III*** in charge of the military.

GODS, BELIEFS AND RITUALS

The gods of the Egyptian pantheon

Paser's sarcophagus

The cosmogonical tales describe how, at the beginning of time, the ordered world was put together. Strangely, no two cities have imagined the same creation process; each one of them makes different primordial gods the main protagonists who coexist without the slightest difficulty. In the holy city of Heliopolis, it is said that from chaos, called Nun, emerged a god, Re'-Atum-Khepri, who created himself. And, he conceives the first divine couple, Shu and Tefenet, representing, respectively, dry and moist air. Out of their union spring Geb, the earth, and Nut, the heaven. The sarcophagus of Paser, who was a priest of Amun at Karnak, illustrates this stage in the creation and shows Shu, his arms raised, holding the slim body of Nut high above that of Geb, resting languidly on the ground. On the right, the deceased looks on, his arms bent before him in a gesture of adoration. Note that he has not neglected to cover his sarcophagus with all the symbols of protection and long life: the ankh, the was scepter, the wedjat eye, the loop of eternity, etc.

Whoever undertakes to study Egyptian religion must start by postulating that the gods exist; but only because the Egyptians have told us that they do. As opposed to monotheistic religions, the reality of the gods is placed on exactly the same plane as that of the universe or of the living beings. Therefore, it is not a question of believing or not believing; it is a fact. Here, faith does not depend on revelation. Thus, one neither accepts nor denies this faith: one admits it.

Furthermore, their purely human status makes the gods mortal. They are born, become old and die in a perfectly natural manner. They disappeared for good, one day, together with the civilization that had created them. Today, these gods have neither priests nor worshipers; they are simply a subject to be studied.

An analysis of the Egyptian pantheon rapidly reveals that its polytheistic nature is its most important feature. In fact, from the Delta to Upper Egypt, there is a wealth of gods and goddesses with a variety of names, images, shapes and appearances. Nothing in the Egyptian religion prohibits the representation of divinities, since they are considered as persons with whom anybody can enter into contact through their image. It must be understood and admitted that humans have invented the gods, but in their conception of creation, designed to explain the universe, a god has created them at the same time as he created the other gods and their images. The idols that they worship are not the gods; they are only images of the gods. The Egyptians knew full well that these statues and portrayals of the divinities were only partial and imperfect representations. Each god has, in reality, several facets. A certain facet is linked to a specific function as well as to a characteristic feature of the god. Inversely, one single image can be used to personify several different gods. For example, the god *Thoth* can be represented by an ibis but also by a baboon, which, otherwise is the major sign for the sun. The gods are shown as animals or humans and, sometimes, as a subtle combination of both. *Hathor* the goddess of music and joy is sometimes represented as a cow, sometimes as a woman with a cow's head, sometimes as a woman wearing a crown with two horns encircling a solar disc. Gods are masculine or feminine, rarely both.

The Egyptian pantheon consists of two main groups: on the one hand, those who are wrapped up (*Ptah*, *Osiris*, *Min*), linked to the underworld or to fertility: on the other, those who can move freely. The latter wear a stereotyped garment: short loincloth for the gods, and long narrow tunic, held up by shoulder straps, for the goddesses. Both gods and goddesses are barefoot. The gods never follow fashion: their apparel is classical and has changed little during the four thousand years of their existence. Therefore, we cannot identify them by their clothing, and if they were not accompanied by their name or some distinctive attribute, crown or scepter, identification would be impossible. The gods are always clothed; nakedness is not permitted except for god-children.

Finally, the gods have a threefold existence: in heaven lives the **ba**, the soul of the god; on earth, his image; in the underworld, his body. The same is true for the humans, which means that the gods rule undisputedly over the three elements that constitute the universe: heaven, earth and **duat**, the world beyond.

Cosmogonies and legends

In the beginning of the world, the gods were created by a demiurge, creator of the universe, masculine or feminine. Then, generations of gods came into existence by entirely natural reproductive processes. Within the large family constituted by the Egyptian pantheon, each member was given a place of residence near relatives or rivals, but this communal life does not seem to have created any problems.

To explain the creation of the world, the great theological schools imagined cosmogonical systems that were as numerous as they were varied and different. Each clan, each city, each province composed a story of the creation around its tutelary deity, which persisted until the extinction of the pharaonic civilization. Of course, some cosmogonies, in which the more influential gods were the main actors, enjoyed greater renown than others that were too specific to gain a large following. Three of them seem to have been special favorites.

According to the Great Ennead of **Heliopolis**, there are nine primordial gods: *"Before the heavens existed, before the earth existed, before humans existed, before death existed,"* there was the *Nun*, a kind of inert primeval chaos. From the *Nun*, the sun Re'-*Atum-Khepri* emerges. He is his own creator because he has come into being by himself: *"When I became manifest to existence, existence existed...,"* he says, *"... because I came before the preceding Gods, because my name preceded theirs because I made the preceding era as well as the preceding Gods."* He is alternatively: *Khepri*, at sunrise, represented by a scarab, **kheper**, which signifies "be born," *Re'*, at noon, when the sun shines, represented by a disc; *Atum*, at sundown, represented as an old man.

It is said that, by masturbating and spitting on the ground, Re'-*Atum-Khepri* gives birth to a divine couple: *Shu*, the domain of the air, and *Tefenet*, moisture. From their union spring *Geb*, the Earth, and *Nut*, the Heavens, who give birth to *Osiris*, *Isis*, *Seth* and *Nephthys*.

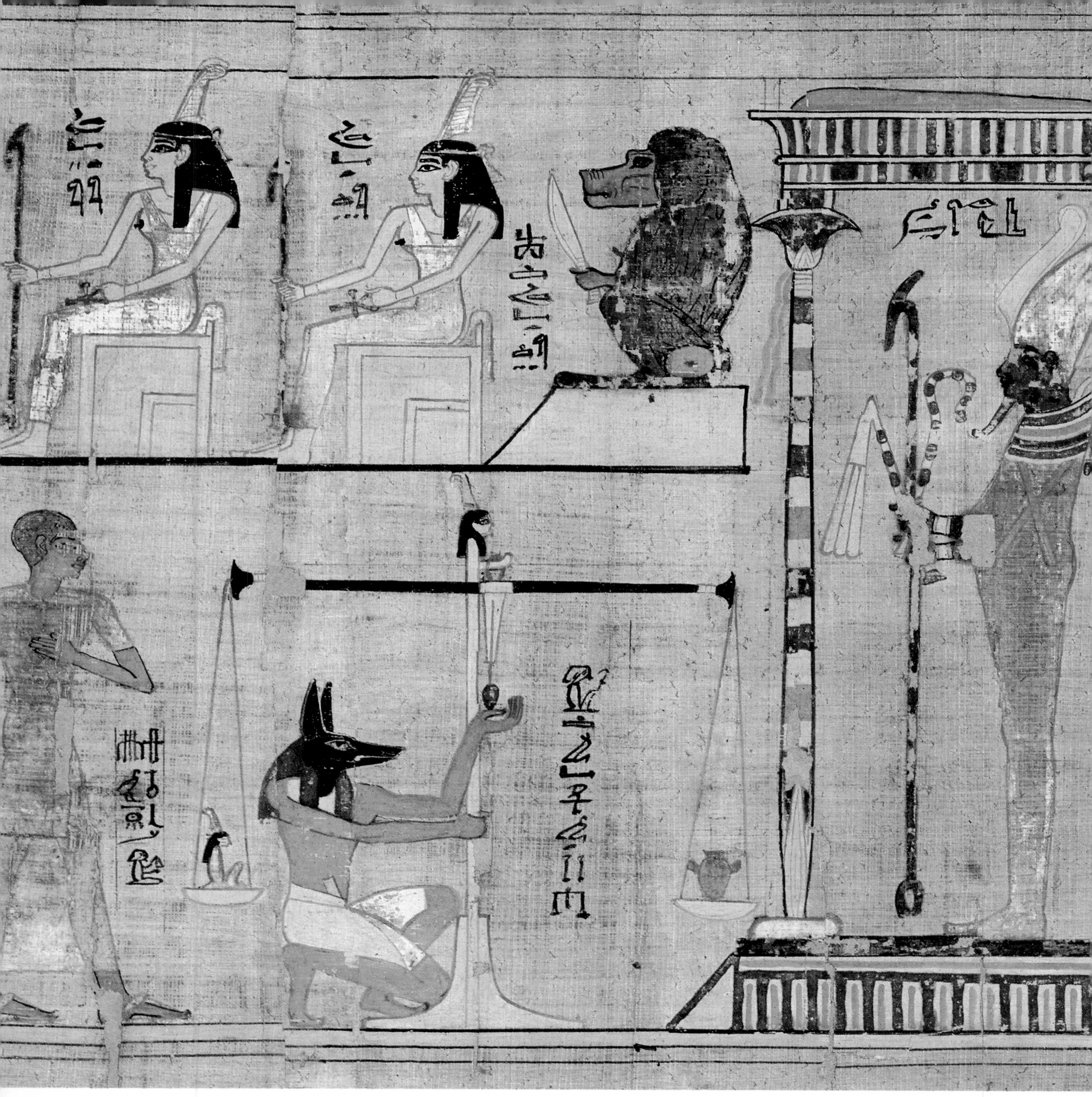

These nine creators guarantee the link between the gods and the humans because the last two generations introduce the reign of the humans, thanks to the **"Legend of Osiris."** This legend is the most famous of all in Egyptian mythology and reached far beyond the pharaonic culture since it was taken up by Plutarch, who added a multitude of details in his work *De Iside a Osiride*.

Everything begins with the reign on earth by *Osiris*, after his father, *Geb*, the Earth, had made him heir to his realm. It is said that he taught the humans to farm and gave them laws and religion. His brother, *Seth*, became jealous and made plans to assassinate him. To this end, he invited *Osiris* to a banquet with forty-two other guests, his accomplices. During the feast, *Seth* brought in a magnificent casket that he had had made to the precise measurements of *Osiris*. He promised to give it to whoever, lying down inside it, fitted it perfectly. Everybody tried but it fit nobody. Finally, *Osiris* lay down in it and filled it exactly. Immediately, all the guests rushed forward to close the casket, which was sealed and thrown into the Nile.

Isis, the sister and wife of *Osiris*, went around the country searching for him, in vain. She finally found him in the port city of **Byblos**, brought him back and hid him in the Nile Delta. There, she succeeded in conceiving a son by him, *Horus*, who grew up hidden by the thick growth of papyrus. However, *Osiris*'s merciless brother *Seth* discovered his corpse, cut it into pieces and scattered the pieces all over Egypt. *Isis* again took up her quest, helped by her sister *Nephthys*, and found all the pieces, except one, the phallus, which had fallen into the Nile and been swallowed by an oxyrhynchos, a fish associated with *Seth*. *Isis* and *Anubis*, the jackal, reassembled *Osiris* and wrapped his body in strips of cloth, thus creating the first mummy. Finally, with the help of *Thoth*, *Isis* brought him back to life, but to a new form of life, since henceforth *Osiris* reigned over the nether world. His son, *Horus*, after a battle with *Seth*, obtained the supremacy of the terrestrial realm from the tribunal of the gods.

Starting with this basic story, theologians added a multitude of secondary legends either to introduce a local deity into the cosmogony or to make several cosmogonies compatible. An example of this is the wonderful legend **"The eye of Re',"** which explains how, one day, it happened that the sun, *Re'*, lost his eye. He sent his children in search of the missing organ. Time passed and, tired of waiting, *Re'* decided to replace the lost eye. Just as the fugitive eye returned and, seeing that it had been replaced, it began to cry. From its tears, **remut**, humans, **remet**, were born. Re' became angry and transformed it into a cobra that he attached to his forehead: it became the **uraeus**, which rises from the royal crown and whose duty it is to strike down and annihilate the enemies of the god. The origin of this legend can only lie in a play on the words meaning "tears" and "humans."

The cosmogony of **Hermopolis** is more difficult to define. We know of it by late, fragmentary Heliopolitan texts, and this presents the problem of the transformations that it might have undergone by being taken over in this way. Here, the original chaos is not described as a total void, because four couples of spirits inhabit and form an indivisible core. The males wear frog heads and the females wear serpent heads: *Nun* and *Nunet* (the primeval Ocean), *Hehu* and *Hehet* (Infinity), *Keku* and *Keket* (Darkness), *Amun* and *Amaunet* (what is Hidden). These eight gods come together to create and deposit an egg on a headland emerging from the water: the Sun. At the dawn of time, the cult of these gods is replaced by that of *Thoth*, a lunar god and divine messenger, who, after having come to life through his own power, presents an egg, the Sun, which he places on the initial headland.

Only one, fairly late document describes the cosmogony of **Memphis**: it is a slate dating from the 25th dynasty, which belonged to a *Ptah* temple at **Memphis**. It combines elements from **Heliopolis** and **Hermopolis** but gives the role of creator to the local god, *Ptah, "the one who made all the gods (...) who created all countries by Thought and Word."* He achieves the creation by the sole activity of his mind, which conceives the elements of the ordered world that he wants to create, and of his tongue, which, by expressing the idea, gives it life.

The gods as protectors of kingship

Represented as a falcon or a man with a falcon's head, *Horus* symbolizes several deities. He is the son of *Isis* and *Osiris*, who has triumphed over his uncle, *Seth*, and received from the hands of *Geb* himself the realm of the earth. This means that Pharaoh, who is of divine essence, is considered as the incarnation on earth of *Horus*, who therefore becomes the main protector of the Egyptian kings. In the royal titulary, two names recall this identification of Pharaoh with *Horus*: the **Horus name** and the **Golden Horus name**.

However, *Horus* is also a heavenly god with close links to the sun-god. He combines the personalities of a multitude of gods, also represented as falcons: *Harakhty*, "Horus of the Horizon," a sun-god worshipped in **Heliopolis**; *Harmakhis*, "Horus on the Horizon," guardian of the gates, who symbolizes the ends of the horizon where the sun appears and disappears; *Haroeris*, "Horus the Great," responsible for the extermination of the enemies of *Re'*; *Hurun*, a god of Canaan origin identified with the sphinx, thus with *Harmakhis* and *Horus*. Moreover, he embodies several other gods because of his family ties with *Isis* and *Osiris*: *Harpokrates*, "Horus the child,"a figure of *Horus*, son of *Isis*, who has remained a child and is shown as a young, naked boy, wearing the childish lock of hair and sucking his finger; *Harsomtus*, "Horus who unites the two lands," who, after having triumphed over *Seth*, unites Upper and Lower Egypt under his single authority; *Harsiese*, "Horus" in his most common form, that of the *Osiris* legend, later made popular by **Plutarch**.

The weighing of the soul

At the end of his voyage in the regions of the underworld, the deceased enters the hall of judgment, where the Tribunal of the gods is in session, presided by Osiris, who, in this papyrus, stands under a canopy; his body is encased in a mummy-like garment and he carries the divine scepters. The decisive stage is the weighing of the soul, when Ma'at, the goddess of truth and justice, is placed in one scale and the heart of the deceased in the other, while the jackal Anubis controls the weighing. If the judgment is favorable, i.e., the heart has the same weight as Ma'at, the deceased is admitted to the realm of Osiris to enjoy the pleasures of a second life in the paradise of afterlife. If not, he is devoured by a hybrid being, called the "Great Devouress," whom the owner of the papyrus, Neferubenef, has obviously not cared to portray here.

Preceding pages

The casket of statuettes of Bakimen

The deceased should bring with him to his last resting place the objects that he will need in the afterlife to insure a comfortable second life. The statuettes, ushebtis, have an important role since they are supposed to carry out the daily chores that will be assigned to the deceased, particularly heavy labor. This type of casket was placed in the tomb near the sarcophagus and destined to hold the figurines. The sides show Bakimen, the deceased, worshipping the two major funerary gods: Isis and Osiris. On the first one, they are represented in a traditional manner: Osiris, with his flesh colored green, is wearing the atef crown with two plumes and carries the heka cross and the flail; behind him stands Isis wearing on her head her own emblem, the high-backed chair. The second side, on the contrary, has a more unusual iconography: the figures are still Isis and Osiris, but here they appear as the goddess Hathor and the falcon-god Horus.

Hatshepsut and the goddess Hathor

Hathor is the great nurturing goddess, the one whose task is to suckle the royal infant in the case of theogamy, the marriage of the god of the kingdom to the Great Royal Wife. In the temple of queen Hatshepsut, Hathor has a sanctuary especially reserved for this essential role of the goddess. Here, she is represented as a cow with the solar disc between her horns; at her feet, the infant Hatshepsut sucks her teat to feed on the divine and sacred milk.

[Temple of queen Hatshepsut at Deir el-Bahri, West Thebes, Upper Egypt.]

The god *Amun* has his origins in **Thebes**, where he began as a minor participant, together with *Amaunet*, in the Hermopolitan cosmogony. He is rapidly promoted and grows in importance, power and influence. At the beginning of the New Kingdom, he becomes a national and dynastic deity and a universal creator. The 18th and 19th dynasties strengthen his power and, above all, that of his clergy, who attain such a degree of prosperity that they form a state within the state. Until the end of the Greco-Roman period, temples dedicated to him are built throughout the country, notably at **Karnak** and **Luxor**, and constantly enlarged and embellished for over a thousand years.

His original personality is difficult to define because, as his popularity grows, he never ceases to borrow the features of other gods. His name means "the Hidden," therefore he must have been a god of the air and invisible space. In his form as *Amun-Re'*, he takes on the qualities of the sun-god from **Heliopolis**. In that of *Amun-Min*, he becomes a god of fertility and creation. When represented as a human, he wears the crown with two high plumes, and his symbolic animals are the ram and the goose. With his companion, *Mut*, and the child-god, *Khons*, he forms a divine triad.

Mut also has her origins in **Thebes**, but is famous only because of her association with *Amun*. She is generally shown as a woman crowned with the skin of a vulture. Later, when *Amun* assumes the character of sun-god, she becomes the eye of Re' and, in this capacity, she is represented as a lioness and war-goddess, but a friendly one. As to *Khons*, the youngest member of the triad, he is the "Wandering one," a lunar god shown as a man with a falcon's head, often wearing a solar disc topped by a crescent moon.

Aten represents, above all, the solar disc. Already in the 5th dynasty, as the cult of the god Re' becomes more widespread, the name of *Aten* is mentioned in the **"Texts of the Pyramids"** to denote the sun's globe. However, it is first in the 18th dynasty, in particular during the reign of ***Amenhotep III***, that the first signs of a cult appear, rather timidly at first. It is ***Amenhotep IV***, better known as ***Akhenaten***, "He who pleases *Aten*," who elevates him, for a time, to the rank of dynastic divinity, thereby ousting *Amun* and, especially, his clergy. He is represented by a solar disc whose rays, ending in hands, carry the cross of life, the **ankh**.

Funerary deities

Osiris , who had inherited the kingdom on earth from his father, had been assassinated by his brother, but later resuscitated by his sister, becomes the master of the underworld. As god of the dead, he presides over the tribunal that decides the fate of the deceased. To begin with, this cult is exclusively reserved for the pharaoh, but during the Middle Kingdom it becomes more accessible and everybody is allowed to identify himself with the god in the afterlife. The tomb paintings show him as man with green flesh, his body encased in a mummy-like garment, wearing the **atef** crown with two tall plumes and carrying the royal scepters, the **heka** cross and the flail, crossed on his chest. The main site of his cult is **Abydos**, in Upper Egypt, where it is said that *Isis* found his head; the faithful were expected to go there on a pilgrimage at least once in their lifetime. In his quality as a resuscitated god, he strives for the annual renewal of the vegetation. At the time of sowing, people made statuettes of "growing *Osiris*" that were filled with silt and seeds: the number of seedlings that came up were supposed to indicate the quality of the harvest in the coming year.

Isis, the sister and wife of *Osiris*, is the most popular of the Egyptian goddesses. Her immense popularity stems from her exemplary behavior in the *Osiris* legend, where she appears as a faithful wife and devoted mother; thus she becomes the protector of women and children. Similarly, her funereal role is fundamental because she is directly involved in the resurrection of *Osiris*, which confers on her the prestige of a great magician. She is represented as a woman crowned by a high-backed chair, the hieroglyphic sign of her name. In the course of time she acquires the characteristics of a number of other goddesses whose iconography she then adopts. Her cult is exceptionally long-lasting in Egypt: her temple at **Philae** does not close its doors until 551 in the reign of ***Justinian***, thereby definitely putting a stop to paganism.

Nephthys owes her privileged place among the gods only to her direct family relationship with *Isis* and *Osiris*. Because she had helped her sister to find the pieces of *Osiris*' body, she has a role of protector and, with her sister *Isis*, she watches over the body of the deceased. On the sarcophagi and in the reliefs she is shown as a woman wearing on her head the hieroglophyic signs transcribing her name.

The jackal *Anubis* is said to have been born of the illegitimate love between *Osiris* and *Nephthys*. He is the unchallenged protector of the cities of the dead and, in particular, he is the god presiding over the embalming ceremonies. He is supposed to have invented mummification. Moreover, it is he who accompanies the deceased into the afterlife and leads him to *Osiris* and the tribunal of the gods, where his soul will be judged. As for *Thoth*, he starts out as a simple moon-god but his functions increase with time: he is, above all, the reckoner, the one who invented the calendar, mathematics and the script. By extension, he becomes the god of wisdom and knowledge, patron of scribes, magicians and physicians. He is the messenger of the gods, the divine scribe, the one who writes down the final decision by the funerary tribunal, as well as the name of the new pharaoh, on the leaves of the sacred tree at **Heliopolis**. He is represented in many shapes: ibis, man with the head of an ibis or baboon. Some statues show a scribe bent over his work with a baboon sitting beside him: this is *Thoth* in his role as patron of scribes.

In the underworld, *Neith* and *Serket* watch with *Isis* and *Nephthys* over the canopic jars, which hold the internal organs of the deceased, and, by extension, over the dead body. However, *Neith*, a woman wearing a shield and arrows on her head, is also the ancient goddess of **Sais** in the Delta and, especially, the demiurge of the city of **Esna**: it is said that she came into being by her own power and then created the sun, exactly like the primordial gods. In this capacity, she appears as a cow carrying between her horns the god *Re'*, whom she has fetched out of *Nun*. As for *Serket*, the goddess with a scorpion on her head, she has the power to cure stings of various kinds.

In the beginning, *Ptah*, whose origin was in **Memphis**, shares with *Sokaris* the role of patron of jewelers, artisans and sculptors. Later on, when he has become the creator-god in the Memphite cosmogony, he occupies a paramount place in the Egyptian pantheon: he takes on the personality of *Sokaris*, the funerary god of **Memphis**, protector of the necropolis, under the name of *Ptah-Sokar-Osiris* and forms a triad with his wife, *Sakhmet*, and the child god *Nefertem*. He is represented as a man encased in a garment from which two hands emerge carrying the long **was** scepter: often the **djed** pillar stands behind him, symbolizing stability and durability. Instead of hair and headdress, he wears a blue skullcap.

Apophis, the giant and malevolent snake, personifies the negative forces and powers that are continually threatening the balance of the universe. Every day he attacks the ship of the sun-god Re' at different points of its journey. He is regularly defeated by *Seth*, helped in his task by secondary deities, whereupon he disappears, only to start again the following day. He therefore symbolizes the permanent threat of a return to chaos.

Secondary deities

Nicknamed "The Powerful" or "The Furious", and worshipped and feared throughout Egypt, the lioness-goddess *Sakhmet* is unleashed during the last five days of the year, called the epagomenous days, during which all Egypt offers up prayers and litanies to her for fear that the annual cycle might fail to return. During this time she receives numerous gifts and offerings aimed at pacifying her. In **Memphis** she is the companion of *Ptah*, but her vocation is quite different in **Thebes**, where she is assimilated to *Mut* as a healing goddess. Thus, a great number of lioness-headed statues of *Sakhmet* were placed in the temple of *Mut* at **Karnak** by ***Amenhotep III***, who is said to have suffered from an incurable illness.

The child-god of the triad, *Nefertem*, wears a lotus flower on his head and takes an active part in the Memphite cosmogony because he is thought to be the primordial lotus from which the sun, *Re'*, emerged.

Min, associate of *Amun*, was worshipped at **Coptos** and **Akhmim** as protector of caravans in the western desert, but he owed his popularity particularly to his role as a fertility god. His appearance is characteristic of his functions: he wears a mummy-like garment, his penis is erect, his right arm (the hand holding a flail) is angled upwards behind his head. He wears a high headdress, identical to that orn by *Amun*. The feasts devoted to him marked the beginning of the harvest. At the start of the season of **Chemu**: he was offered lettuce, whose juice was supposed to be an aphrodisiac.

Khnum is a god with a ram's head who reigns in several areas and has different functions according to his place of residence. At **Elephantine**, he associated in a triad with a companion, *Satis*, and a child-goddess, *Anukis*. The Egyptians believed that the flood came from an underground cavern, near the first cataract, where *Khnum*, *Satis* and *Anukis* reigned. Every year, at the time of the flood, they released from the reserves, stored up by *Ha'py*, the amount of silt needed to fertilize the arable land. At **Esna**, where he is associated with *Neith*, as well as at **Antinoe**, where his wife is the frog goddess *Heqet*, *Khnum*, the creator-god, models gods and humans on his potter's wheel.

The god *Ha'py* personifies the Nile, the flood and the inundation. He is the symbol of plenty and is presented as an androgynous figure, sometimes female, sometimes male, obese and with pendulous breasts. He enjoys great popularity all throughout Egyptian history and receives constant offerings to persuade him to vouchsafe the country a sufficiently abundant flood. The flood, marking the beginnings of the Egyptian year, is also called "the arrival of *Ha'py*" and is celebrated with feasts in his honor. At the base of the temple walls, he is shown in processions of figures personifying the countryside, presenting offerings of produce to the master.

"The Powerful One"

No Egyptian divinity has as many faces as Sakhmet, the lioness-goddess. She is nicknamed "The Powerful One" and reputed to be a manifestation of the eye of Re', who pursues and destroys the enemies of the sun. Both feared and respected throughout Egypt, she is the incarnation of all forces of destruction: she is responsible for incurable illnesses, wars, epidemics, etc. She does, however, know how to cure all these ills since she also appears in the shape of healing goddesses such as Mut, for example, and protects the corporations of physicians and veterinarians. In that quality, her main sanctuary was at Memphis, where she was associated in a triad with Ptah and Nefertem. However, her reputation seems to have spread rapidly across the borders of this city, since she appears in most sanctuaries in the Nile Valley, including later monuments from the Greco-Roman era.

[Upper Egypt.]

Nut, the vault of heaven

The goddess Nut belongs to the Great Nine, the Ennead, of Heliopolis. This cosmogony, constructed by the Grand Priests of Re', features nine primordial gods in order to explain the creation of the world. Nut symbolizes the vault of heaven and forms a divine couple with her partner, Geb, the earth. Neither one has a specific cult place, but, they often appear in funerary representations describing the journeys of the sun-god, Re', or on cosmogonical papyri. It is said that Nut swallowed the sun every evening and returned it to the world early the next morning. This is why she is shown as a female figure with an elongated body stretching from East to West, across which the stars and the constellations travel.
[Valley of the Kings, West Thebes, Upper Egypt.]

Nekhbet and *Wadjit* are tutelary goddesses of the "two lands". *Nekhbet*, the vulture-goddess from **El-Kab**, protector of Upper Egypt, is a woman with the head of a vulture, or simply a vulture who spreads her protective wings over the king. *Wadjit*, the cobra-goddess from **Buto**, is the protector of Lower Egypt, the cobra whose role it is to destroy the enemies of Pharaoh.

Originally, *Hathor* is a heavenly goddess often represented as a cow. Her name signifies "the house of *Horus*," and she symbolizes the celestial space through which solar *Horus* travels. Theologians rapidly make her a daughter of Re' and it is in this quality that, in case of a divine marriage, her role is to suckle the royal infant. In time, her functions grow more numerous: she becomes goddess of sweetness and joy, protector of the necropolis at **Thebes** or goddess of the fig tree at **Memphis**. Already during the New Kingdom, she is identified with *Isis* and is then represented as a woman wearing a headdress composed of two stylized horns encircling the solar disc. Traditionally, *Horus* is her husband, but her popularity among the faithful stems mainly from her role as protector of women giving birth and new-born babies.

Bes, the bearded, bow-legged gnome with coarse, jolly features is one of the best-loved gods because of his function. He is said to watch over the home and to chase away evil spirits by his terrible grimaces and grotesque dances. It seems that he has no particular sanctuary especially devoted to him, but he enjoys great favor among the common people, lasting well into the Christian era. This is also true for *Taweret*, called "The Great One," and considered as the goddess who protects women and children. She is recognizable by her rather startling anatomy: the body and head of a hippopotamus, the back of a crocodile and lion paws.

Bastet embodies the peaceful qualities of dangerous goddesses, such as *Sakhmet* and *Tefenet*. She is a joyful goddess with a friendly disposition, represented as a woman with a cat's head and carrying a sistrum in her hands; or, more frequently, simply as a cat. Considering the great number of necropolises of sacred and mummified cats found in Egypt, her cult must have been very popular. She is also said to be the eye of *Atum*, acting as a moon-goddess who watches over pregnancies and births.

Ma'at, is considered to be the daughter of Re' and personifies the truth, justice, universal order and cosmic balance that were intended to prevail in the world after its creation. It is by her powers that the ordered world maintains its integrity. The gods depend on her, and offerings to *Ma'at* constitute one of the fundamental rites of daily religious observance. Everyone must respect what she represents in order to insure the regular return of the natural phenomena that guarantee life. When the deceased's heart is weighed, she is placed in one of the scale-pans to measure the weight of his wrongdoings. She is shown either as a woman wearing an ostrich feather on her head or simply as an ostrich feather, the hieroglyph that signifies her name.

Seth, represents, by himself, all the ambiguities of the divine. He protects the solar ship against the serpent *Apophis* but he is also the malevolent god who killed his brother *Osiris* and who, one way or another, is a source of trouble and disorder. The Ramesside dynasty, with its origins in the city of *Seth*, attributes a particular importance to him, sometimes going as far as integrating his name, although spelled differently, into that of certain pharaohs, the ***Sethos***, for example. However, from the Late Period onward, he comes to symbolize the Foreigner and, by extension, the Invader; he becomes hated and rejected and his name and effigies are destroyed.

Montu is a falcon-god from **Thebes**. He is the incarnation of irresistible force in battle and enjoys great favor, especially from the Middle Kingdom on, when Egypt begins to plan extensive territorial conquests. The pharaohs of the 12th dynasty build several temples in his honor. The most famous is the one at **Tod** where, in 1936, an Asiatic treasure was found bearing the name of ***Amenemhet II***, which contained rough lapis lazuli, gold and silver objects, amulets, cylinder seals, chains, cups, etc.

Although there were many cults of sacred bulls in the country, that of *Apis* was the most popular. In **Memphis**, he was worshipped as an incarnation of the god *Ptah*, but he is also associated with *Osiris*, which is the reason why he figures among the funerary deities. The sacred bull, chosen because of certain markings on his hide, gets a magnificent funeral when he dies. From the New Kingdom onward, mummified bulls placed in great basalt sarcophagi are deposited in the **Memphis Serapeum**.

Rituals and beliefs

Egypt has always been dominated by an acute awareness of death and a constant preoccupation with life after death. No other people can boast of having devoted so much effort to death and, especially, to survival after death. This does not in any way mean that they were attracted by death; quite the contrary, because they thought that *"death is a painful event, a source of tears and sorrow."* Their dearest wish was indeed to live to the age of one hundred and ten years and enjoy a protracted old age. Although the Egyptians believed that only the gods could grant life and death, no special divinity symbolized death: it was treated as something unjust. The Egyptians feared and rarely appreciated death but they knew that it was inevitable. They undoubtedly loved life on earth but realized that it was ephemeral; life after death, on the other hand, was eternal, and one should therefore prepare oneself for it as well as one possibly could. Nothing must be overlooked in the careful planning of a beautiful funeral, and it was quite natural to spend one's life making all the necessary arrangements for a smooth transition of the soul into the afterlife, in the best possible conditions and insuring that its eternal resting place was properly built.

According to Egyptian thought, every human being is composed of different elements, some spiritual and some material. The spiritual elements include: **sekhem** and **sakh**, the spiritual energy and body; **akh**, the invisible power, but especially **ba**, the soul, and **ka**, the sustaining spirit. The **ba** is the spiritual part of the person that leaves the body as death takes over; it then recovers its individuality and can roam at will. It is represented in the form of a bird and can stay close to the body in the funereal chamber, but it can also wander quietly outdoors to revisit favorite haunts of the deceased, whom it somehow "represents." The **ka** is more difficult to define because there is nothing in our ideas or our languages that corresponds to this notion. It is a manifestation of vital energies that both conserve and create, capable of surviving physical death. The material elements include the body, **khet**, the heart, **ib**, and the name, **ren**, which exists as a second creation of the individual. The Egyptians have a deep belief in the virtue of the name: to name a person is equal to making him or her live beyond the physical disappearance of the body. This is why the name of the deceased is written so many times in his tomb or funerary temple.

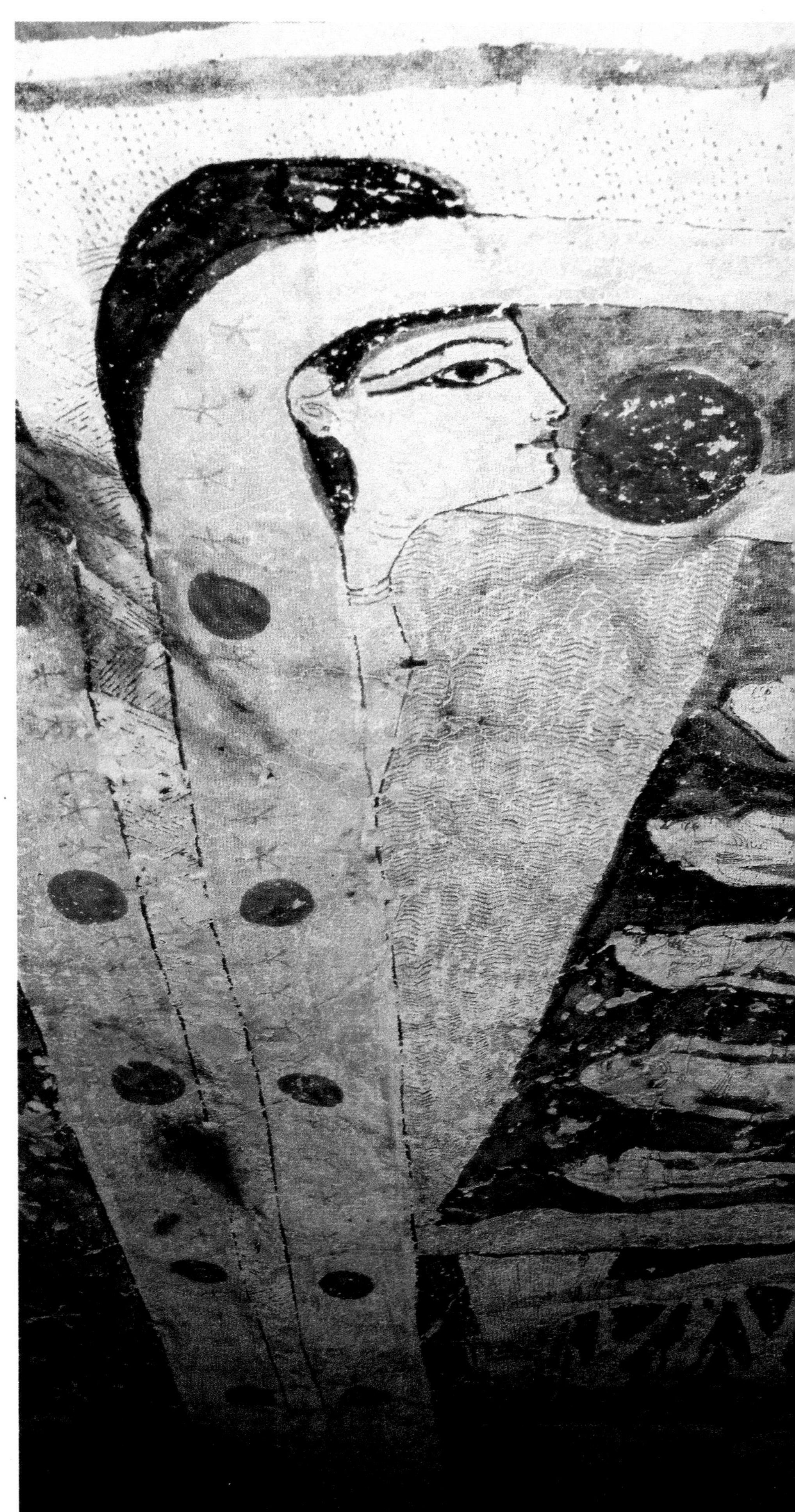

The spirits of the Nile

This androgynous deity, endowed with pendulous breasts is called Ha'py: it personifies the flood and the inundation, fecundity and abundance, thus by extension, the Nile. Most Egyptian temples are decorated with friezes showing Nile gods kneeling and holding in their out-stretched arms trays heaped with all kinds of produce from the fertile earth. In addition to the funerary temple of Sethos I, the site at Abydos includes a small, less well-known sanctuary, built during the reign of Ramesses II. Unfortunately, it is very damaged and only the foundations have withstood the robbers. On the remaining walls are lists of the royal domains and the provinces of Egypt, all of them personified by Nile gods.
[Temple of Ramesses II, Abydos, Upper Egypt.]

Mummification

We know that for the Egyptians death is not an end, but a transition to another form of existence. This transition is necessarily fraught with danger because, when death occurs, the different constituent parts of the human personality disperse, although, individually, each one of them retains its own integrity. If one succeeds in reassembling them, the second life is possible. To manage this, one has to preserve the most vulnerable element, the body. If it is left to deteriorate, every chance and all hope of survival are lost. Embalming is the only way of conserving the body. The practices of embalming, carried out by great specialists, are recorded by **Herodotus**.

"First, they extract the brain through the nostrils with an iron hook but in this manner, they only take out part of it; they dissolve the rest with certain drugs. Then, using a sharp stone, they make an incision in the side and empty the body of its entrails; they rinse this cleaned-out cavity with palm wine and powder it with aromatic substances; then, they fill the belly with pure, crushed myrrh, cassia and other known aromatic herbs except incense; finally, they stitch it up."

All that is left now are the skin, the bones and the cartilages, which must be dried to avoid putrefaction.

"They steep the body in salt by immersing it in natron for seventy days. When the seventy days are past, they wash the mummy and then, wrap it completely in strips of very fine gauze, drenched in the gum that Egyptians generally use instead of glue."

The strips are sometimes several hundred meters long, as each member is wrapped individually before the whole body is finally bandaged. When he winds the body, the embalmer puts protective amulets in prescribed places: the **wedjat** eye, the **djed** pillar, the **knot of Isis**, gold finger-stalls, etc. The heart is put back after having been mummified. Similarly, the viscera are treated separately, according to the same embalming techniques, and placed in the four canopic jars provided for this purpose, under the protection of the **four sons of Horus**.

Beliefs and funerary cults

In a country where religious beliefs vary from one city to another, it is to be expected that the doctrines concerning the afterlife should vary accordingly. In the course of the centuries, the various beliefs develop, become enriched and transformed, finally ending up as hybrids with links to each original one but without possessing all the characteristics of any single one.

To begin with, the prevailing idea is that the deceased, buried in the sand, will come back to life in the hereafter. It therefore seems perfectly natural and vital that he should have something to eat in his new life; hence the importance of depositing food offerings. Whatever grave is chosen in whatever period, the problem of food seems so predominant that it may appear as a paralyzing fear of "going without." Through the centuries, the civil iconography evolves: certain themes disappear in favor of others, more adapted to the new conditions in the country. A single feature persists, immovable and unchanging:

the funerary banquet, often exceedingly lavish. The deceased is shown sitting at a table groaning under the victuals: all seems set for a second life of abundance.

This initial, persistent belief is enriched by two new elements at the end of the Old Kingdom: that of *Osiris* and that of the sun-god *Re'*. *Osiris* is the master of the underworld and, at the end of his journey the deceased is give a parcel of land in his realm so that he can continue his earthly activities. In the **"Fields of Iaru,"** he plows, sows, harvests: this is reassuring but exhausting. Therefore, the work is entrusted to the figurines, the **ushebtis**, who are meant to carry out the chores in the dead person's stead. As to the sun-god rituals -reserved solely for royals during the Old Kingdom and subsequently extended to their subjects- they consist in conducting the deceased into the domain of the sun to accompany Re' on his journeys. Here, all the incoherences of this survival concept become apparent: the deceased is at the same time in the heavens journeying in the solar ship, under the earth in the **"Fields of Iaru,"** in his tomb enjoying the food and even, if he so desires, back on earth visiting his favorite haunts. A solution had to be found that was more appropriate and less constraining. During the day, the deceased is in his tomb, enjoying the offerings and sometimes, taking a short walk on earth; at night, he accompanies the sun-god on his voyages, stopping for a while in the **"Fields of Iaru,"** at dawn, he comes back to rest in the calm and cool of his tomb.

One part of the funerary cult is the obligation to keep the deceased provided with fresh food offerings. Obviously, this can be done by the direct descendants of the dead person, but it becomes much more of a problem as the generations go by and the number of cults increases; hence the creation of funerary funds. The system consists in attaching a property to the tomb with a sufficient revenue to provide the deceased with food and the funerary priest with a salary. Initially, this custom was created for the king, who fed his subjects, but it could exist only if the royal family was very rich and the beneficiaries fairly few. Very soon, everybody wants to establish his own funerary cult. Prosperous people keep the tradition of a property fund and appoint a priest to their own cult. However, as the properties are inherited and divided up, the practice of offerings is gradually abandoned. It is followed by a more efficient system: a contract between the owner of the tomb and a priest stipulates that the fund must be inherited, undivided, by only one of the priest's sons. To guard against any mishaps, some also try to take advantage of the funerary offerings made to the gods. By royal consent, they place one of their own statues inside the temple of the god and can then enjoy the left-overs when the god has eaten his fill.

However, in spite all these precautions, the Egyptians do not appear to have been very optimistic about the durability of their funerary cults: they could see, in their own lifetime, how old graves were abandoned and frequently looted. This showed the importance of resorting to magic to insure access to the afterlife. To make an object exist, it was enough to represent it and to name it. Representing it was not a problem: the tombs are full of pictures of food, but somebody still had to come and recite the magic spells to make it exist.

Following pages

The "Book of the Dead"

This painting is taken from the "Book of the Dead" of Khonsumes who, in the Low Period, was the controller of finances in the temple of Amun at Karnak. This funerary book, written on papyrus, contains the entire one hundred and ninety chapters aimed at insuring the survival of the deceased in the afterlife. Dressed in a wide linen robe with a cone of perfume on his head, the deceased makes a libation of water and offers incense to four gods, who stand facing him: Harakhty, sun-god with a falcon's head who is one of the many figures of Horus; Osiris, wearing the crown with two tall plumes and carrying the divine scepters crossed on his chest; the goddesses Isis and Nephthys, each crowned with the hieroglyphic sign of her name.

SOCIETY, PEOPLE AND SCIENCE

The different social classes

Karomama

The Divine Women Worshipers of Amun were very influential because they were thought to be the earthly wives of the god. In this capacity, they acted as counselors to the king, enjoyed numerous privileges and owned huge estates. Karomama was, doubtlessly, a granddaughter of Osorkon I and reigned as undisputed sovereign of Thebes during the 22nd dynasty. She is shown here wearing a dress with a pattern of bird wings and advancing regally with outstretched arms. She probably carried two sistra, now lost, which were a type of rattle whose tinkling calmed the gods. The workmanship of this bronze statue, inlaid with precious metals, is remarkably delicate and reflects a certain female ideal both in the harmonious lines of the body and in the sweetness of the face.

The complex structure of Egyptian society is the result of the basic concept that its monarchical regime has a divine origin. Pharaoh, chosen by the gods or legitimate son of the gods, is the representative of the gods on earth. Consequently, he wields absolute power which nobody can question: he is head of state, head of religion and commander-in-chief in times of war. However, he is incapable of discharging all these duties on a daily basis. He therefore relies on various institutions that are self-governing but still remain under the constant control of the royal authority. The government, the clergy and the army are the three main centers of power. To head them, Pharaoh appoints directors with the responsibility of managing, in the best interest of the king, the different departments of their institutions. They are, in the main, diligent and conscientious men who enjoy a number of advantages: income from property rents, large salaries, royal gifts and donations, etc.

Next in the Egyptian hierarchy come the various corporations, fairly privileged because they regularly receive royal bonuses. They are the scribes, the priests and the craftsmen. It is true that they depend entirely on the institution that employs them but, compared to the lower civil servants, they enjoy a higher social standing and better salaries.

Finally, at the bottom of the social scale, there are the peasants, crop or cattle farmers, working for the state or for some private individual. They have no possessions and can be exploited at will. They are the underclass of Egyptian society.

This highly hierarchical and severely regulated society is remarkable for its continuity throughout Egyptian history: for three thousand years, no major change intervened to upset the initial order.

Viziers and nomarchs

The Egyptian word **tjaty** designates the magistrate who is the unassailable head of the executive power and the whole administrative system, a sort of prime minister. In English, there is no ready equivalent, so we will call him **"vizier."** As the guarantor of moral order, he wears his emblem, a small figurine of the goddess *Ma'at*, on his chest. During the Old Kingdom, Pharaoh appoints a single vizier but, after the territorial expansion of the New Kingdom, he needs three viziers who share the management of the kingdom: the viziers of Lower Egypt, Upper Egypt and the "Head of the South," **Nubia**. The vizier is chosen from among the best scribes in the country and becomes the most important person after the pharaoh: he is *"the will of the master, the eyes and ears of the sovereign."* The function is a difficult one and during the ceremony of investiture the king never fails to warn his future vizier: *"Behold the chamber of the vizier. Watch over everything that must be done there because it is there that the existence of the whole country is safeguarded. Assume the office of vizier; watch over everything that is done in its name because the whole country relies on it. To be a vizier is not pleasant; it is as bitter as bile."*

The competence of the vizier extends over all sectors: justice, agriculture, irrigation, army, police, public order, granting of land, control of personal ambitions, taxes, finance, levies, inspection of royal storehouses, reception of foreign ambassadors, appointment of civil servants, membership of the war council, etc. Frequently, his day starts early by a confidential meeting with the king to inform him of the state of affairs in the country and ends late after numerous interviews, conferences, perusals of reports and records, journeys of inspection, etc.

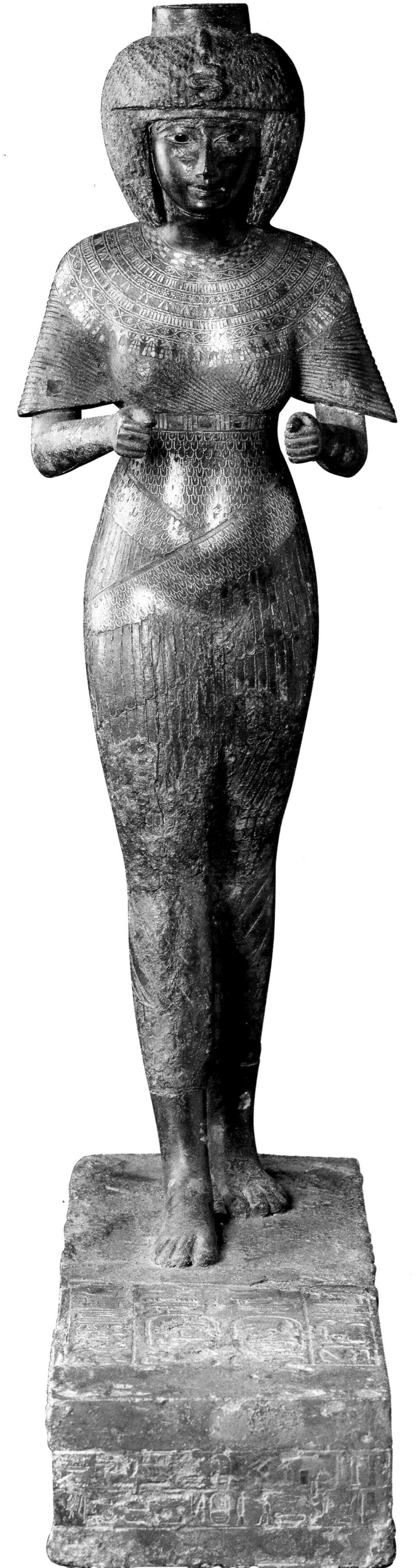

In return, the prestige is proportionate to the work load. The rich tombs and elaborate titularies of viziers such as **Ptahhotep**, **Ty** and **Mereruka** of the Old Kingdom, **Rekhmire**, **Ramose** and **Keruef** during the New Kingdom, give ample evidence of their important role in the Egyptian government.

The **justice** department, somewhat on the margins of traditional government departments, had a rather original structure. In theory, Pharaoh is in charge of settling quarrels among his subjects according to the laws and maintaining the order established by *Ma'at*, the goddess of justice and truth. In practice, he delegates his judicial powers to the vizier, who insures that the rule of law is upheld throughout the country. The process of law is quite cumbersome and painstaking but precise and rational in civil matters: the time limit for contesting a decision varies from two days to two months, depending on whether the plaintiff lives in the city or in the country. However, in criminal matters the process is much more forceful: interrogation by means of a cudgel is a generally accepted method.

Magistrates and courts of law are numerous and omnipresent. From the "Officer of village quarrels" to the great Courts of the Royal Residence, justice is meted out. Common cases are tried by local administrations. Otherwise, the case is recorded by a clerk of the court and the plaintiff and accused are then called in to solve the dispute. However, the law suits are often protracted, the possibilities of appeal are countless and the adjournments for inquires and deliberations are frequent. For crimes closely connected with the interests of the state, whether it is grave robberies, stealing of sacred or cult objects, attempts on the life of the king or insults to the royal person, the heavy judicial machinery is set in motion: extraordinary courts, presided by Pharaoh, are convened to pronounce sentence.

In addition to the existing and frequently applied laws, rules are gradually established on the basis of previous, often quite ancient, judgments. The records of court proceedings are conserved for a very long time in the drawers of the "Royal Archives" and serve as examples to the lawyers: it is the beginning of a true jurisprudence. For minor offenses, theft, larceny, libel, small embezzlements or administrative abuses, the punishments are beatings, twisting of the feet or hands, mutilation of the body, forced labor or deportation. For more serious crimes, vigorously repressed by the law, the death penalty is mandatory but, fortunately, rarely imposed: the condemned is thrown to the crocodiles, impaled or burned. When a high official or a member of the royal family is implicated in a serious crime, he is encouraged to commit "suicide," because, contrary to those who are condemned to death, deprived of all hope of survival, suicides are not excluded from the afterlife or from the realm of *Osiris*. In fact, the guilty person is simply walled up alive. In any case, whatever the nature of the crime, the king must confirm every death sentence, and he is the only one who has the right to grant a pardon.

Regionally, it is the **nomarchs** who head the administration of the province entrusted to them. When the country was unified, Pharaoh divided it into provinces called **nomes**, organized on the basis of irrigation, breaking of new land and agricultural productivity.

During the Old Kingdom, the hereditary principalities of the thirty-eight Egyptian provinces eventually destabilize the regime, which is already terribly undermined by the weakened royal authority. The estates become feudal strongholds and their lords strive to acquire the privileges exclusively attached to the royal domains: they declare themselves independent and collect taxes for their own benefit. In response, the Theban kings of the Middle Kingdom conserve the same administrative division but create more, and therefore smaller, **nomes**, grouped together for economic reasons into vast territories that are carefully controlled by the central government. The vizier abolishes the right to inherit official positions and appoints military commanders to govern each province.

In the course of three thousand years, the number, the names and the borders of these provinces have changed due to various economic, social and political factors, but despite these changes, the **nome** remains an economic and fiscal unit. In the late period, the royal scribes count forty-two provinces in Egypt, but one must question whether this number is not directly related to the forty-two gods who sat with *Osiris* on the funerary tribunal. Each **nome** has its own pantheon of gods, its temples, its laws and its taboos. Whoever settles in a given province must undertake to respect the rules and regulations obtaining there.

Sitting scribe

He is commonly called "the sitting scribe" because, today, we have no way of knowing with certainty who he was, where he lived or even in what period. This statue of painted limestone represents a scribe, sitting cross-legged with his scroll of papyrus on his lap, ready to take dictation. In his right hand he probably held a calamum, a sharpened reed, or a brush, which is lost. His face, animated by eyes inlaid with crystal and quartz, set with copper, still expresses the concentration of a scribe at work. Like all members of his profession, he has chosen to be portrayed as pleasantly plump because, in ancient Egypt, to be able to eat well was a mark of high distinction.

The clergy

Because of their sacred function, the **clergy** form one of the dominating classes in Egyptian society. Their role, however, is neither to be spiritual guides nor preachers: they are the servants of the god who lives physically and materially in the temple, not only as a statue, but often in the shape of an animal as well. The god is a living being, vulnerable and with the same needs as a human. The role of the priest is to maintain the statue, and especially its occupant, in good health: dress it, care for it and protect it against any outside influence that might diminish its power.

By their presence and their activities, all Egyptian temples, whatever their cult, must help to maintain the universal order and safeguard creation, failing which the world will return to primeval chaos. The king is the cornerstone of this world harmony, symbolized by *Ma'at*, and by virtue of this quality, he is the only one worthy of officiating in the temple. The priests serve only as delegates of the king: in the name of Pharaoh, the legitimate heir to the divine kingship, they carry out the necessary daily acts of worship in the temples, but the king alone figures on temple walls performing the various rituals in front of his peers.

The members of the staff entrusted with the running of the temples belong to different categories, each with a rigid hierarchy. First, there are the administrators and the auxiliary personnel. The former are ordinary civil servants, who may be very numerous in the larger temples. They are responsible for the economics of the temples: control of tax collection, management of the estates of the god and of his treasures, relations with associated temples and with central government. The latter are the scribes, craftsmen, policemen, guards, farmers and gardeners whose task it is to maintain the temple, as well as singers and musicians whose performances are a necessary part of the religious ceremonies. All of them are dependents of the temple but not specifically part of the clergy.

Then come the high clergy with, at its top, the "servants of the god," called **hemu neteru**, who were erroneously described as "prophets" by the Greeks because they sometimes had to interpret the will of the gods. At the head of any given temple is the First Prophet. The priest who occupies this post in the great temple of *Amun* at **Karnak** is one of the most influential individuals in all Egypt. This category also includes the "divine fathers," the "pure," the **kheryhebet**, who keeps the program of the ceremonies inscribed on a scroll, and the members of a college of grand priests, the **unuyt**. The lower clergy are lumped together, without distinction, in a group of auxiliary priests, called the "purifiers." In secondary temples, they sometimes perform the rituals, but in the larger ones they only carry out material tasks. As opposed to the higher clergy, they are not permaent members of the profession. They are divided into four classes or **phyles** who manage the temple for one month each. The same team returns only after an interruption of four months, so that they work only three months of the year. The rest of the time they carry on with their usual activities.

Finally, there are the "specialists," who are closely linked to the temple but can have independent occupations. They are the "scribes of the House of Life," who compose and copy out the mythological inscriptions and sacred texts used in the cult, read them out during important ceremonies and can even, on royal orders, represent the clergy of a given temple, the "scholars," and the "horoscopes" that determine the auspicious and inauspicious days of the year.

The most serious obligation imposed on the priest is to maintain the purity of his body because he officiates in the "house of the god." He is required to wash twice a day and twice at night, according to **Herodotus**. He must have his face and head clean-shaven, all other hair pulled out, and be circumcised. During his period of service, he must abstain from sexual relations and obey all the rules pertaining to food and religion obtaining in the **nome** where he works. He eats neither mutton, nor pigeon, pelican, pork or fish. Vegetables such as garlic, onions and beans as well as oil, wine and salt disgust him and make him ill. He must be dressed in simple pure linen cloth and sandals of palm fibers. His bed is a thin woven mat that he spreads in the courtyard of the sanctuary. If he takes a wife, he must remain monogamous. He is afraid of journeys: he thinks that in foreign countries, hostile powers and the forces of chaos dwell. It is understood that his physical purity is accompanied by the knowledge required to perform the sacred duties. In fact, his knowledge is vast. He is a subtle theologian, a good architect, a sound mathematician, a proficient astronomer; but he also practices medicine and magic.

Thoth watching over Nebmertuf

This shale sculpture comes from the temple of Thoth at Hermopolis. It shows Nebmertuf, scribe and chief of the lector-priests under Amenhotep III, beside a baboon perched on a pedestal who represents the god Thoth. Here, the "Master of divine words," in his quality as patron of the scribes, watches over Nebmertuf, who is bent over his papyrus scroll, listening to the god and preparing to faithfully write down the divine words. Statuettes of this type, found in great numbers, constituted offerings or ex-votos to the divinity whom one petitioned for favors.

The army

As soon as the pharaonic state was formed, Egypt acquires a well-organized military system controlled by special scribes who carefully manage supplies, recruitment and postings. However, the actual organization of the **army** obviously develops in accordance with the changing objectives of Egyptian military policies.

Under the **Old Kingdom** the pharaohs do not conquer any new territory and no foreign invasion threatens the country. If, for some reason or other -to collect booty or defend a border- it becomes necessary to rapidly raise an armed force, it is the duty of the nomarchs to levy the best people among the local population as long as the operation lasts.

The standing army has few regulars, essentially specialists, organized into a very rudimentary structure. They accompany peaceful or economic expeditions and guard the great building sites. They are divided into three specific units. The "elite recruits" guard the palace and insure the policing of the desert. The "specialized units" have various duties: some are responsible for *"spreading the fear of the King in foreign countries"* and *"reporting things that are ornaments to the King;"* others, recruited among the best linguists, travel to the **Country of Punt** in **Nubia** or to **Byblos** to collect rare materials; others again, accompany and protect the caravans that bring back to Egypt the precious minerals extracted from the quarries. As for the "guard units," they watch over the great royal construction sites in the cities and maintain public order in the country at large, *"in such a way that nobody strikes his companion, nor snatches the bread dough or the sandals from a passer-by, nor steals clothes in any village, nor steals a goat from anybody."*

The expansionist policies of the **New Kingdom** make it necessary to set up a permanent and professional army which becomes a separate, privileged and powerful social class. Its prosperity is due to the distributions of booty, tax exemptions, rewards and gifts from Pharaoh: when a soldier has particularly distinguished himself on the battlefield, he receives "The Gold of Bravery" as well as a gift of "good land," which often provides him with quite a comfortable income. The power of the army is such that, at the end of the 18th dynasty, while the country is still suffering the after-effects of the Amarnian schism, the highest-ranking general becomes king of Egypt: *Horemheb*, then *Ramesses I*, are both military officers elevated to power by the army. In theory, Pharaoh, assisted by a War Council, is the supreme commander of the armies. If he cannot direct the operations himself, he delegates the command to his senior general, assisted by lieutenants who transmit the orders to the commanders and officers. Certain remote military regions, far from the capital, are put under the direct command of these lieutenants and the "royal commissioners for foreign countries" carry out small-scale military operations, particularly along the national borders.

The army is very heterogeneous, composed of foreign mercenaries, Egyptian volunteers and captives; if it is not large enough, Pharaoh assumes the right to recruit, from peasant families, the men he needs to achieve his aims. For great battles and territorial conquests the structure requires a combination of two armed forces. The infantry, which is the less prestigious, is organized into sections and companies making up four divisions of five thousand men each, under the protection of their own particular divinity. The chariot army, a much nobler force, is divided into squadrons that surround and protect the divisions of foot soldiers. It consists of five thousand chariots, i.e., around ten thousand men. The navy does not fight, although its role is essential to the army as it manages transport, provisions and supplies.

In spite of the prestige and power of the the army, the daily life of the soldiers, particularly of the poor foot-soldiers, does not appear to have been either comfortable or glorious. One only has to consult the **"Satires of the trades,"** a text highly appreciated by the masters of scribe-schools, to understand the horrors, ignominy and humiliations that the future warriors had to contend with.

"Take his advance into Palestine, his campaign on the dunes, with his food and his water on his shoulders... He drinks brackish water and only stops to stand guard... Does he reach the enemy? He is like a trapped bird without any strength left in his body. Does he return to Egypt? He is like worm-eaten wood, he is ill, he must take to his bed and he is carried off on a donkey! His clothes are stolen and his companion runs away..."

The bowl of Djehuty

This solid-gold bowl was given by Tuthmosis III as a reward to general Djehuty, one of his closest associates. It is said that the clever general had succeeded in taking the city of Jope by hiding his men in large jars. The bowl is designed as a pool of water with floating papyrus heads and fish swimming around a central rosace.

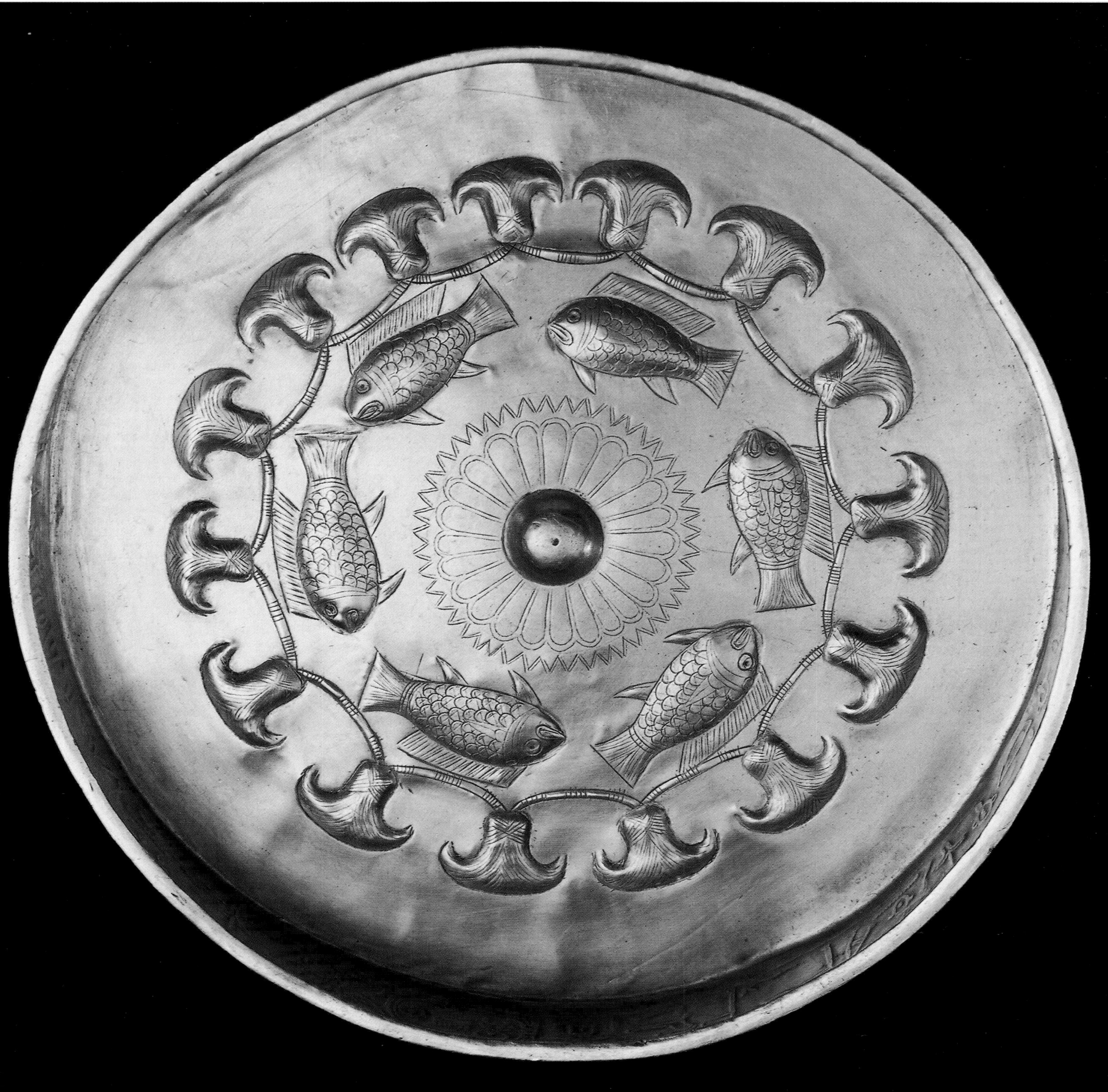

Scribes and craftsmen

"See, there is no state that is not dominated apart from that of the scholar who himself dominates... It is the scribe that sets the taxes for Upper and Lower Egypt and it is he who collects them; he does the accounts for all that exists. All the armies are dependent on him. He ushers the magistrates before the pharaoh and determines the step of everybody. It is he who commands the whole country; every matter is under his control. His profession is the highest of all professions." In fact, whether as the grand **scribe** of the Royal Household or as a small provincial secretary, it is a great honor to exercise this profession because, of all men, it is he, the scribe, who manages everything. The literal translation of the Egyptian word that we translate by "scribe" is, in fact, "the one who writes." All those who handle the reed, whether they compose sacred texts or books of wisdom, draw up cadastral lists or update work logs, belong to the same fraternity whose patron is *Thoth*, the divine scribe.

From the Middle Kingdom on, the need to train great numbers of scribes in order to reform the administration of the country leads to the establishment of national education programs for children of the same age. For the child destined to become a scribe the studies are exacting and difficult. He starts his schooling at three years of age. He is taught to read, write and count at the same time as the moral rules governing society are instilled in him. He distinguishes himself by his good behavior and his culture; he is pleasant and knows how to speak in turn, respects the laws and the established order; he remains modest and self-controlled. Independent thinking and personal ideas are not encouraged: he should abide by traditions and ancient experience. He is first taught the hieratic, or type of cursive, script and particular attention is paid to the correct spelling of words: place-names, foreign names, technical, military and other terms. Moreover, the child must be able to calculate swiftly and correctly, assess a tender, design a building, evaluate a surface area; this knowledge he acquires by frequent sessions in the field. Sometimes, the study of foreign languages is required: Caanean, Cretan, etc.

Any strategy that makes the child work is acceptable: compliments, competitions, threats, corporal punishment, promises of a magnificent future or, simply, selected reading of, among others, the popular **"Satires of the trades,"** a collection of texts whose purpose is to prove that only the profession of scribe is worth pursuing.

"I have seen the worker in the mine laboring in front of the furnace. His fingers made one think of a crocodile and he smelled worse than fish offal. The stone mason finds his work among all sorts of hard stones. If he has accomplished it, his arms are worn out and he is tired. When he sits down at dawn, his thighs and his back are broken...

I tell you, regarding the mason, he is more despicable than words can express in a room measuring ten cubits by six. The shoemaker is in a very bad way, he is constantly begging. What he eats is leather. The laundry man washes on the riverbank next to the crocodile. I then tell you how it is with the fisherman, he is more miserable than any other profession. Is his work not on the river where he mixes with the crocodile?"

The profession of scribe is attained through assiduous studying and there is no lack of positions in the government. However, the hierarchy is cumbersome and consists of many levels: a subordinate scribe may be a simple copyist, a brilliant one may reach the highest offices in the land. Their role in society is of such importance that, unavoidably, they enjoy numerous privileges bestowed by the king: exemption from taxes, various presents, gifts of land, etc. There are many portrayals of scribes at work, both in paintings, sculptures and engravings. The hieroglyph designating the profession is a scribe's palette composed of two small cups: one for the red pigment, the other for charcoal black. A calamus-holder and a water pot complete the equipment. The medium preferred by the scribe is papyrus, which can be rolled without breaking, but as a scratch-pad he mostly uses shards of pottery or limestone, called **ostraca**.

The Egyptian language does not differentiate between the words for **artist** and **craftsman**: both are designated by a hieroglyph representing a metal tool used to drill a hole in a stone vase. This means that there is no clear boundary between the two professions because, in Egypt, our modern notion of art for art's sake is inappropriate. In fact, everything is created not to be beautiful but, primarily, to be useful. The craftsmen strive to be efficient and productive. When building temples, carving out tombs, making statues, their duty is to help the humans achieve immortality while making reality eternal.

Today, if certain objects are considered as masterpieces, it is because the Egyptian craftsman has succeeded remarkably well in his work: he has known how to depict the real nature of his subject for the sole purpose of portraying life so as to make it last. Egyptian art is the result of a need to conserve life, beyond the physical body, and the will to immortalize thought. From this point of view, it seems perfectly natural that the author does not sign his work. However, the craftsman knows his worth and is conscious of his skill and perception. In biographical notes inscribed on the walls of his tomb, he explains that he knows how to *"render the movement of a man walking as well as that of a woman advancing, the attitude of a trapped bird, the lunge of a man knocking down an isolated prisoner while his eye fixes his opponent and the face of the enemy is convulsed by fear."*

The guild of the craftsmen comprises all manual workers although some trades have a higher standing than others. On the one hand, there are the carpenters, shoemakers, porters, brewers, potters, wood and leather-

The sign-bearer

In the reign of Amenhotep III, civil art attains an exceptional degree of refinement, proving that the artists have achieved total mastery of their materials. Whatever the medium (wood, semi-precious or ordinary stone, glazed pottery, bronze, etc.), the result is exquisite; it displays a multitude of details in the shaping of the body, the treatment of the hair and the crowns or the folds of the clothing. This sign-bearer perfectly illustrates the high level of artistic achievement. The figure, doubtless a high official, holds in front of him a pillar supporting an effigy of the god of the kingdom, Amun-Re', represented as a ram wearing the solar disc on his head.

workers, launderers, weavers, etc. On the other, we have precious-metal smiths, jewelers, sculptors and engravers who, judging by the quality and wealth of their tombs, seem to have had very comfortable incomes. The great majority of the craftsmen divide their day between the large state manufactures and their own workshops where they do their personal work. The most skilled are attached to a temple, palace or royal workshop because, although the great building projects are subjected to certain conventions and are carried out collectively, the sovereign always knows how to appreciate, honor and reward outstanding individual talent.

The peasants

"It is certainly true that these people are, at present, the ones who work the least to obtain a harvest... When the river has come of its own accord to water their fields and, having accomplished its task, retreats again, everyone scatters the seed on his land and releases his pigs. By trampling the ground, the animals bury the seeds and the man only has to wait for harvest time and, when his pigs have crushed the ears on the threshing floor, bring in the harvest."

In spite of this description by **Herodotus**, the life of an Egyptian peasant is not as easy as all that. From times immemorial, Egypt owes its prosperity to the strenuous labor of its farmers. They work unstintingly on the land despite the fact that it does not belong to them and that the society they feed hardly leaves them enough to survive. Over the centuries, their living conditions and lifestyle have changed very little. By contempt for the rural world and to give their pupils a lasting distaste for farm work, teachers do not hesitate to paint an exaggeratedly sinister picture of the peasant condition.

"Mice are plentiful in the fields, locusts descend, cattle devour and the orioles bring dearth to the farmer. What remains on the threshing floor attracts thieves, its market value goes down, the team of oxen dies of exhaustion from trampling the corn and pulling the plow. Then the scribe lands on the riverbank; he comes to collect the tax on the harvest, accompanied by guards armed with cudgels and by Nubians carrying palm fronds. They say: "Give us the grain!" although there is none. They beat the farmer who finds himself bound and thrown into the well, head first. His wife is strangled under his very eyes, his children are tied up. His neighbors abandon him..."

Everyday life at Deir el-Medina

Among the sites where ordinary people lived, none is better known than that of **Deir el-Medina**, and it gives us an idea of what daily life was like in a pharaonic Egyptian village, although **Deir el-Medina** is really quite a special case in the administrative organization of the country. **Deir el-Medina** means "Convent of the City," referring to the monastery established in the Ptolemaic sanctuary of the goddess *Hathor* there, in the 5th century A.D. Its ancient name was **Set Ma'at**: the "Place of Truth." It contains the homes of the craftsmen working on the tombs in the **Valley of the Kings** and the **Valley of the Queens**.

Several thousand **ostraca**, pottery shards or bits of limestone, found among the ruins of the houses or in wells, give detailed information of life in the village, of how the work was going, of judgments, crimes, various transactions, inheritances, strikes, etc. This is, without a doubt, a major documentary source for the Ramesside period. The village of **Deir el-Medina** was founded by ***Tuthmosis I*** and originally contained sixty houses, but it was abandoned in the Amarnian period, later to be repopulated in the reign of ***Horemheb***. It reaches its peak in the Ramesside era: one hundred and twenty houses harboring some one thousand two hundred people. At the beginning of the 21st dynasty the community dwindles, after five hundred years of existence.

Champollion discovers **Deir el-Medina** in 1828, but between 1860 and 1910, the necropolis is completely abandoned to the grave robbers: men like **Lepsius** do not hesitate to cut out entire walls of the civil tombs to bring them back to Europe. There are one thousand three hundred graves of varying sizes, constructed by the craftsmen in their spare time.

The workmen are paid to excavate, construct and decorate the royal tombs. They must live in perfect isolation since they know better than anybody where the tombs are, how they are built and what they contain. The craftsmen are put under the direct authority of the vizier of **West Thebes** and kept under strict surveillance by Nubian militia and police. Nevertheless, despite all these precautions, it seems that the inhabitants of **Deir el-Medina** were often involved in cases of grave robbery during the Ramesside period.

Woman carrying offerings

The civil necropolises of the First Intermediate Period and the Middle Kingdom have yielded up a number of "models": statues that are, in reality, transpositions of the paintings that, during the preceding periods, decorated the walls of the funerary chapels. They are usually made of wood or painted limestone and compose entire scenes of daily life, or recount the various stages of the burial ceremony of the deceased. The woman carrying offerings symbolizes the estates of the deceased. In this role, she arrives carrying on her head and in her hands jars and bottles containing all sorts of beverages and foodstuffs belonging to the deceased.

In Year 16 of the reign of ***Ramesses IX***, and from the Year 19 of ***Ramesses XI***, the authorities organize several series of trials to punish the guilty, but, above all, to stamp out grave violation forever by making the sentences extremely severe. From the proceedings of these trials, it emerges that, in most cases, craftsmen from the royal building sites served as informers and active accomplices or simply, stayed silent and impassive while the night-time raids went on, for fear of being assassinated by the robbers.

The village is divided by a central lane into two sections. To the East lives the team of the right, to the West the team of the left. Each team is headed by an architect or a contractor. It is made up of several scribes, draftsmen, painters, engravers, sculptors, masons, miners, plasterers, porters, laborers and apprentices. The royal scribe serves as the link with the administrative authorities: he records, in the "official diary of the Institution," the accomplished tasks, the general progress, what materials are used, the wages, the incidents as well as important daily events: feasts, births, marriages, funerals, the death or accession of a king, visitors, etc. He makes the daily roll-call and notes absences, which are always due to more or less dubious causes: *"Brewing beer; His mother has come to visit; Building his house; Burial of the god; Offering to the god; Making pills for the scribe's wife; Is with his god; Has a sore eye; Making Hormes' mummy; Stung by a scorpion"* and, of course, the very useful, accompanying his superior, which remains the most frequent excuse for not being present on the building site.

The work is organized into sequences of ten days, during which the workmen stay on the building site, which is near the **Valley of the Kings** and equipped with seventy-eight sleeping huts. Everyone rests for a day every ten days, and feast-days are free. The royal administration supplies food and water from the storehouses and **chadufs** of nearby temples, among others, the **Ramesseum** and **Medinet-Habu**. Wages are paid in kind: wheat, bread, cakes, fish, vegetables, fruit, beer, milk, oil, fat, fire-wood, clay pots and clothes. However, in the Ramesside period, rationing and wage problems provoke the craftsmen of **Deir el-Medina** to organize the first strike in history. The conflict begins in Year 29 of the reign of ***Ramesses III*** and lasts until the end of the Ramesside era: *"Twenty days have past in the month without our rations being given to us,"* the workers explain. Thus, on several occasions, they leave the building site and occupy the temples of **West Thebes**.

The most entertaining texts are those written by the workmen themselves, totally unofficial writings, personal reminders, etc. Here, we find, expressed very simply, all human failings: corruption, adultery, libel, theft, denunciations, cheating, and so on.

"To make known what I have had to pay the superiors of the craftsmen to enroll my son in the team. These things were mine alone and nobody else's. To the head of the team, Nekhtenmut: a leather bag worth fifteen copper debens. To the head of the team Inerkhau: wood for a small armchair worth thirty copper debens. To the scribe Horisheri: a large wooden folding chair worth thirty debens and a foot-stool." The enrollment of the son in the team cost almost as much as seven kilos of copper, i.e., around seven months of his father's work!

The life in such a closed community was conducive to robbery, adultery, theft, revenge, crime, etc. The most notorious known example concerns a man named **Amenonah**. He was accused of robbing the tomb of ***Ramesses III***, but the case was dismissed and he was released for lack of evidence. He had stolen, all the same, and when archeologists uncovered his grave, they found the object in question hidden inside.

Notions of Egyptian mathematics

Few texts make clear the extent of the Egyptians' knowledge of mathematics. At most, one can try to estimate it from the monuments that they built. Integers are represented by a system that is both decimal and additive. Each power of ten: one, ten, a hundred, a thousand, ten thousand has a different hieroglyphic sign. The numbers are written from left to right. Zero does not exist, but certain scribes leave an empty space to indicate its presence. With such a system, additions and subtractions remain simple. For multiplications and divisions, the multiplier or divisor is decomposed as far as possible so that the calculation is reduced to a simple addition. The Egyptians knew the square and square root of certain numbers; this makes it easier to measure surface areas and volumes. For the fractions, they only know those whose numerator is one, with the exception, in later periods, of two thirds, three fourths, four fifths and five sixths.

Like their arithmetic, their geometry has practical objectives: calculate the surface area of fields, volumes of buildings or pyramids. Their strong point is that they have a recipe for calculating the surface area of a circle as a function of its diameter. This means that they use a value of π of 3.16, which is quite a remarkable approximation. To sum up, it must be emphasized that in Egypt, mathematics were practiced entirely for utilitarian purposes, which contrasts with the much more abstract and objective view of mathematics prevailing in Mesopotamia.

The sciences

Astronomy, astrology, magic, botany, mineralogy, medicine, mathematics, geometry, physics, etc. It is clear that no science is neglected in ancient Egypt. Various catalogues and treatises, carefully written down on papyri or **ostraca** or on the walls of the temples reveal the extent of the scientific knowledge of the Egyptians. Among all the countries of the ancient world, the Valley of the Nile is considered to be the cradle of all knowledge, hospitable to all scientists and scholars curious to explore the mechanisms that govern nature and the ordered world.

By "science," we mean any specialized knowledge in whatever field: the cosmos, animals, plants, nature, the human body, etc. All these disciplines, strongly influenced by religious beliefs, have one thing in common: their development is always linked to a purely practical need. In Egypt, there is no pure research: mathematics and geometry are needed to build pyramids and temples, astrology and astronomy to determine the calendar and the religious feasts, medicine and magic to help the body to survive both on earth and in the afterlife.

However, a careful study of the texts shows that the research rarely turns up any "laws" but, rather, "recipes" intended to solve a particular problem, carry out some building project, treat a disease. Similarly, numerous documents reveal, with great simplicity, the limitations of Egyptian scientific knowledge. For example, when a physician seems totally at a loss to treat a case, he does not hesitate to conclude, after the examination and description of the symptoms: *"... A disease for which nothing can be done."*

In Egypt, disease is very often thought to be due to hostile powers and adverse spirits that have to be treated by magic. The same is true for scorpion-stings and snake-bite, against which it appears that no remedy was ever used, whereas a great number of papyri appeal to healing spirits, particularly the goddess *Serket*, to fend off the venom.

Princess Nefertiabet

Nefertiabet was probably a daughter of king Khufu, and this brightly colored stela comes from the mastaba built for her at Giza. The scene shows the princess wearing a clinging dress of leopard skin, sitting at a table laden with offerings. The text gives an exact list of all the products and their quantities. There are, among others, incense, oil, animals, green and black cosmetics, figs, apricots, bread, fabrics, beer, etc. to enable Nefertiabet to survive in the afterlife.

Side by side with the magicians, a very well organized body of physicians with a strict hierarchy practices a much less primitive type of medicine. There are general practitioners and specialists: ophthalmologists, dentists, surgeons, even veterinarians. Interns or professors are generally attached to an institution of some kind: royal palace for the best of them, army, ministry, etc. We have a great deal of information about the medical knowledge of the ancient Egyptians because many papyri dealing with the subject have survived: various treatises and accounts of analyses, practices, treatments, drugs, etc. One might imagine that the practice of embalming would have made the physicians familiar with the anatomy of the human body but, strangely enough, this is not so. They do not know of the existence of the kidneys, link the stomach to the lungs and the lungs to the heart. The theory of the vascular system is the basis of medical science and all practitioners rely on it. They believe that the heart carries in its arteries every type of liquid present in the body, from the blood, which seems reasonable, to the tears, urine and sperm, which is less so. The medical books give impressive lists of common diseases: ulcers,

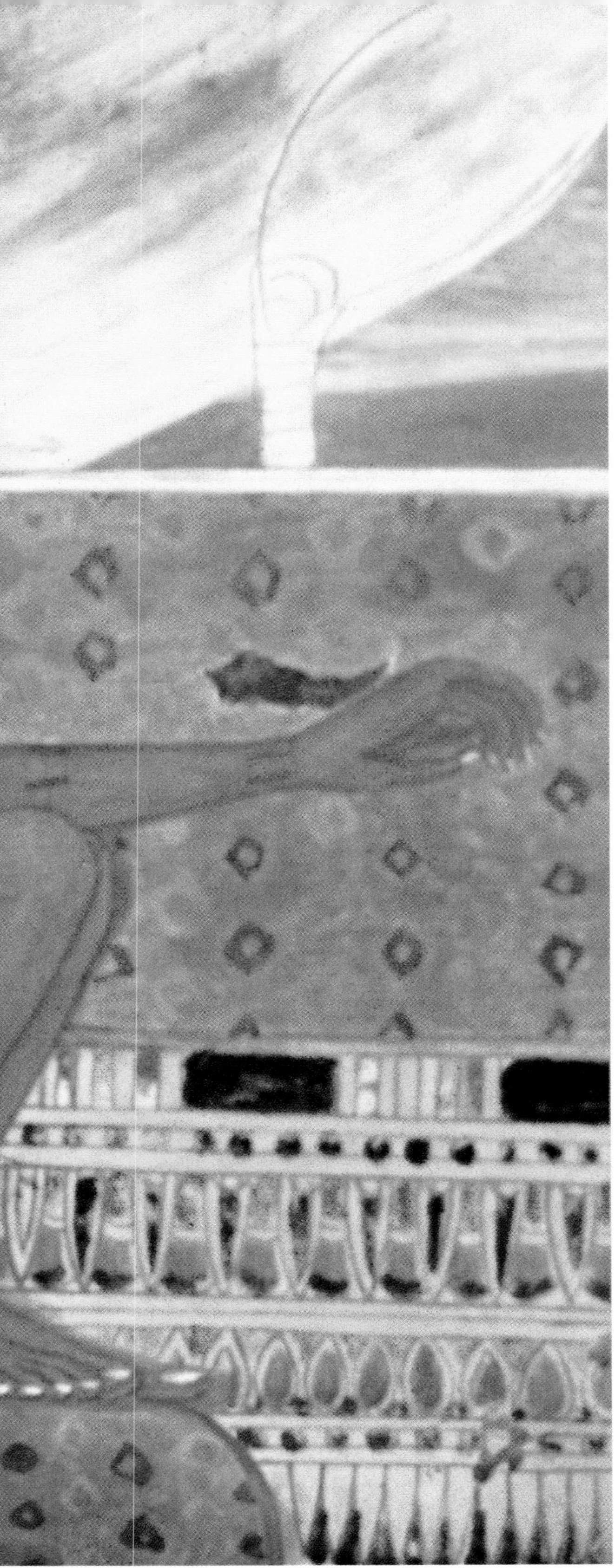

hemorrhages, vomiting, cancers, bilharziasis, constipation, urinary and respiratory disorders, eye trouble, migraines, intestinal worms, etc; and no less impressive lists of suggested treatments: massage, dressings, potions, suppositories, poultices, gargles, pills, ointments, eye-drops, inhalations, and so on. As part of any course of medication, which must not appear too simple or too ordinary, it is fashionable to prescribe remedies consisting partly of medicinal or healing herbs and partly of substances of animal origin, even excrement. According to the texts, fecal matter, dung of donkeys, dogs, antelopes and pigs or, quite simply, "fly shit that clings to the walls" are used to prepare these potions. A good poultice must contain lizard blood and pig's teeth, rotten meat, stinking fat and milk from a woman in labor. In dentistry, the Egyptians fill teeth with a mineral cement and pierce abscesses by drilling through the jaw. However, it is as surgeons that the Egyptian doctors excel. The **Edwin Smith** papyrus lists forty-eight cases of fractures or other problems that are studied with astonishing scientific rigor.

*"**Title**. Instructions relating to such a case. **Examination**. If you examine a man presenting this or that disorder and if you observe such and such a symptom, you should act as follows... **Diagnosis**. Concerning this matter, you should say: a man who has sustained such an accident; a disease that I will treat. **Treatment**. You should apply a dressing or a massage..."*

No matter how rudimentary Egyptian medicine might appear, it must be admitted that, quite often, the prescribed remedies seem to have been, on the whole, effective and appropriate.

Astronomic ceilings, heavenly charts, all kinds of treatises and tables of night-time constellations give an idea of the interest that the Egyptians devoted to **astronomy**. This is again a case of science developed for practical purposes. To establish the different phases of the calendar, divide time, determine auspicious and inauspicious days or place religious constructions and temples in relation to the cardinal points, it is necessary to observe the stars with precision and regularity. They found five planets in the sky which they called *"the stars that know no rest"* and a great number of constellations or groups of stars, unfortunately quite difficult to identify because of the imaginative way in which they are represented: the maps of the heavens are tangles of animals, heavenly gods and goddesses, crowned with colored stars or solar discs, sometimes accompanied by a short caption mentioning their name and characteristics. Nevertheless, all astronomical phenomena, except eclipses and, perhaps, meteors are totally ignored by the Egyptian astronomers. An example of this is the person who, under ***Tuthmosis III***, describes as something inexplicable, incredible and terrifying the appearance in the sky of a "shining celestial body" which, according to experts, might well have been Haley's comet.

The little princesses from Tell el-Amarna

In Tell el-Amarna, the capital of Egypt under Akhenaten, an original style of art develops that differs in all respects from the traditional canons. Apart from the extreme physical deformation of all the figures, the subjects are quite original since they are very often rather intimate scenes of royal daily life. This painting is an example: two of Akhenaten's daughters, completely naked, touch each other's faces in a gesture of pure affection.

THE TOMBS,

TREASURES OF PHARAOHS

From pyramids to the Valley of the Kings

Funeral mask of Tutankhamun

Although we have a rather precise knowledge of the funeral rites in ancient Egypt, we are still uncertain of what types of objects went into the tomb with the sovereign because most royal tombs have been looted, ever since the most distant pharaonic era. Tutankhamun is an exception because his is the only tomb from the New Kingdom found intact. In this period, the country was at the height of its power. The most magnificent objects in his vast treasure were placed in the funerary chamber where the pharaoh was laid to rest. Coffins nestling inside each other contained the royal mummy whose face was covered by this amazing solid-gold funeral mask inlaid with precious and semiprecious stones. It is one of the most expressive portraits of the young Tutankhamun who is crowned with the nemes, wears the false beard and, on his forehead, the symbols of Upper and Lower Egypt, the vulture-goddess Nekhbet and the cobra-goddess Wadjit.

It is called the "Country of the tombs" because from North to South, there is a succession of isolated tombs, necropolises, rock-cut graves and pyramids. There are thousands of them, from simple holes cut into the rock to vast royal funerary monuments. However, the word "tomb" is used generically here as no graves are alike. The most one can say is that there are prototypes that evolve with the centuries according to a number of different criteria. The period, the traditions, the region, the local gods and the social status of the person are among the factors that intervene to modify the ideal grave. The only constant is that the quality, even the existence, of the tomb depends on the status of its owner. The graves of the poor are simple holes dug in the desert sand, where a few utensils have been placed around a low-grade mummy. The rank of the individual in Egyptian society determines the geographical location of his tomb as well as its size, complexity, beauty and, above all, its wealth. As to Pharaoh, he has the privilege of a unique tomb such as nobody else can aspire to.

During the first two dynasties, there is no real difference between the graves of the kings and those of their subjects. Both belong to the **mastaba** type, a flat-topped structure of mud brick whose entrance is marked by a simple funerary stela recalling the names and titles of the occupant of the grave, whether a pharaoh, a member of his family or a private person. At the beginning of the Old Kingdom, ***Djoser*** starts a radical new fashion in royal tombs: assisted by the scribe **Imhotep**, he invents a new form of funerary monument, the pyramid, which is later copied by a number of his successors.

From now on, only the king aspires to a future life with the sun; the civilians only come back to their second life in their tombs, where they then remain. Pharaoh's prestige resides in his divine nature, and after his death, a new life is bestowed on him because of the care devoted to his funerary monument. Even the shape of the pyramid has a "magical-religious" significance. According to the Heliopolis doctrine, after his death the king joins the sun-god Re' and becomes one with him; he ascends to heaven by means of a flight of stairs or by the rays of the sun. The pyramid could therefore be interpreted as a symbolic representation of the stairway leading to the sun.

The funerary complex of Djoser

On the desert plateau of **Saqqara**, on the western bank of the Nile, the bank of the dead for the ancient Egyptians, stands the funerary complex of ***Djoser***, the founder of the 3rd dynasty. The constructions here are so innovative that it seems as if suddenly all ancestral traditions have been abandoned in favor of different concepts, more suited to the new status of the pharaoh: he becomes a god among humans and is determined to show it. Two basic elements characterize this profound change: the use in funerary constructions of the pyramid shape and the replacement of mud bricks by cut stone. The origin of this type of tomb goes back to the pile of sand with which the bodies were covered in pre-dynastic days. However, the idea of adapting it to royal requirements emanated from the famous **Imhotep**, ***Djoser***'s vizier and architect, made a god during the Late Period because of his immense wisdom. In the center of a wide avenue, bordered by a wall, stands the majestic pyramid, and arranged around it, all that is needed to make the soul pass successfully into the afterlife: courtyards and halls, chapels, storehouses for statues and offerings, ceremonial buildings, etc. Everything has been provided to insure the survival of the king.

Preceding pages
The Pyramids of Giza
On the Giza plateau, a few miles south of Cairo, stand the funerary complexes of Khufu, Khephren and Menkaure, pharaohs of the 4th dynasty. Each one of the three compounds includes a mortuary temple destined to receive the body of the deceased on the day of his funeral, a rising ramp, a high temple devoted to the funerary cult of the king and a tomb, the pyramid, sealed on the day of the funeral. In front is the pyramid of Menkaure preceded by small subsidiary pyramids for the queens and princesses. Then comes the pyramid of Khephren, recognizable by its "crown," which is, in fact, a remnant of the original limestone casing which, in Antiquity, covered the sides of all these monuments. Finally, at the back stands the First Wonder of the World, the pyramid of Khufu: it is 2,400 square feet and 475 feet high and is built of some two million three hundred thousand cut stones.
[Pyramids of the 4th dynasty, Giza, Lower Egypt.]

Sethos I and Hathor
This bas-relief is taken from the tomb of Sethos I at Thebes, in the Valley of the Kings. It was given to the Louvre museum together with the sarcophagus of Taho by Champollion who, on this occasion, wrote to his brother: "They are presents that I am giving to the Louvre, where they will remain in memory of me." *For Champollion, it was* "the most beautiful colored bas-relief of the royal tomb," *and it cannot be denied that it is superb. One only has to examine the careful workmanship of the hieroglyphs, the wigs and the clothing to be convinced of its exceptional quality. It shows Sethos I, whose name is written above his head, receiving the magic necklace from the hands of the goddess Hathor. They are holding hands to symbolize the link between the destiny of Pharaoh and that of the divine world.*

Djoser's pyramid is built entirely of limestone and shows successive modifications that are obvious signs of the trial-and-error beginnings of this entirely new departure in Egyptian architecture, at the beginning of the Old Kingdom. Initially, **Imhotep** imagines a colossal **mastaba**, beneath which there is a very deep well giving access to a tomb with a small funerary apartment next to it. It is rapidly enlarged toward the east to house members of the royal family, and eventually topped by a four-tiered structure. Later, supposedly to make it more visible, two additional steps are added which give the finished building the air of a six-step pyramid measuring 200 feet in height. Joined to the north face and closed on all sides lies the **serdab**, a small room that contains a statue of the deceased and whose only communication with the outside is through two cylindrical holes placed at eye level, to allow the king to participate in the offering services celebrated in his funerary temple. As to the other buildings, mostly terribly damaged when they were discovered, they have been the object of major archeological investigations directed by the Frenchman **Jean-Philippe Lauer**. The information collected in the course of his explorations has allowed him to piece together the various elements of the vast funerary complex.

King Sneferu

Three pyramids are inscribed with the name of the founder of the 4th dynasty, ***Sneferu***: one at **Maidum**, the most doubtful, and two at **Dahshur**, the most amazing. In fact, it is most likely that the oldest one, the pyramid at **Maidum**, belongs to his father, ***Huni***. At least, it is thought that he began the construction that his son was to complete. Be that as it may, the solution chosen here shows the new constraints imposed by the evolution of the pyramid tomb: to build even higher and with a steeper slope. It is certain that the architects would have liked to construct the perfect pyramid, but aware of their lack of expertise, they chose a middle way: a building with eight steps crowned by an elegant limestone casing, giving the finished structure the appearance of a real, almost 300 feet high pyramid. It is not known whether or not this result was finally achieved as nothing is left of the upper part. Some believe that the pyramid collapsed even before the construction was finished, no doubt because the planned casing was too heavy. However, graffiti found close by explain that the pyramid did, in fact, collapse, but much later, during the 18th dynasty.

The pyramids at **Dahshur** mark a new and significant stage. The most ancient one, generally called the "rhomboid pyramid" has an original feature: its slope changes suddenly halfway up. Egyptologist s are still puzzled by this and some believe that it is due to the premature death of the king: the work had to be speeded up so that ***Sneferu*** could be buried in his pyramid since this is the only one that can, with certainty, be attributed to him. Others incriminate the **Maidum** pyramid; having realized that it was unstable, the engineers are thought to have abandoned the idea of creating the perfect pyramid to avoid problems.

Finally, with the "red pyramid," the long-awaited goal is reached for the first time: Here is the perfect pyramid. However, despite this feat, which cannot be ignored, a closer examination of the monument reveals its shortcomings. It is clear that some technical problems have not been solved. Its slope is 10° less steep than ***Khufu***'s pyramid; therefore, since the base is roughly the same, the pyramid of ***Sneferu*** is around 130 feet lower, which makes it more squat and less elegant.

The Giza plateau

Here is the site of the most famous royal necropolis of the 4th dynasty. In addition to the three pyramids and their annexes, it contains a great number of tombs harboring high dignitaries of the 4th and 5th dynasties. The king's funerary complex is similar to that imagined by ***Sneferu*** and totally different from that of ***Djoser***. During the burial ceremony, the body is received into the valley temple that stands on the banks of the Nile, at the edge of the cultivated fields; this temple is the point through which it must pass on its journey to its eternal dwelling. The entrance to the valley temple is through a gate leading to a courtyard bordered by chapels and storehouses. It is here that the body is received and purified and where the deceased will be reborn by means of the rituals carried out during mummification to continue his life in eternity, helped by the sacred statues placed in his shrine. An ascending, covered causeway leads to the mortuary temple, also called the high temple.

It is situated on the east side of the pyramid and divided into two parts: first, the antechamber and the courtyard, for the cult of the statues; then the personal temple for the food offerings. Behind it stands the most important component of the funerary complex: the pyramid, the actual grave where the deceased is laid to rest for ever. Pits cut into the rock at the foot of the pyramid contain wooden funerary barges. They are of varying sizes and shapes and destined to allow Pharaoh to navigate in the beyond by the side of his father, the god Re'. In serried ranks, all around the royal monument, lie the graves of civilians whose afterlife is limited to their tombs but who hope that, by being near Pharaoh, they will be included in his life with the sun-god. Those of the highest nobility are buried close to the pyramid whereas the less distinguished have to be content with the edges of the plateau, on the fringes of the desert, thereby respecting the prevailing social hierarchy even after death.

It seems like a strange irony of fate that we know nothing about the greatest builder of all times. Apart from the writings of **Herodotus**, who recorded a more than two thousand year old oral tradition, no document relating to ***Khufu*** has reached us, except for a small ivory statuette, 8 centimeters high! A sad fate for the man who built the First Wonder of the World. He is the son of ***Sneferu*** and ***Hetepheres*** and borrows his father's ideas when building his own funerary monument. More daring and doubtlessly more ambitious than his father, he surpasses anything achieved before to construct a perfect pyramid, 2,500 square feet and 475 feet high with a perfectly regular slope of 52°. The whole structure consists of some two million three hundred thousand cut stones, each around 35 cubic feet, covering 567,000 square feet of land. The facing of rose-colored limestone from **Tura**, partly ripped off during the Moslem Period, would have made the pyramid pointed and perfectly smooth. The absence of the facing, particularly at the top, explains why the pyramid is only 445 feet high today.

The interior arrangements of the monument still cause debate among experts, as they appear to have been altered several times. Initially, there was a small underground cavity to which a long, narrow, sloping corridor gave access. Even before the project was finished, it was abandoned in favor of a chamber built into the masonry and erroneously called the "Chamber of the Queen," which also remained unfinished due to a further change of plans. Then, it was decided to prolong the corridor leading to the second, abandoned, chamber by adding an impressive and spacious gallery, 150 feet long and 27 feet high, ending in a small granite hall topped by an in0ous structure intended to deflect the thrust of the stones above: the burial chamber of ***Khufu***. The whole structure is amazing and shows a perfect mastery of architectural techniques and construction methods that remain a mystery to this day. How did the Egyptians manage to build such a monument? This question has yet to be answered, although technicians, engineers and egyptologists from the four corners of the world have been asking it for years. Theories include an ascending ramp, an encircling ramp, sledges with or without rollers, use of the Nile flood or of a wooden machine resting on a system of counterweights: it seems as if every possible solution has been imagined to explain how the stones were brought to the pyramid and hoisted from one step to another.

Unfortunately, nothing recorded in the historical texts nor imagined by pure reasoning allows us to favor one assumption above another. At the most, in view of certain techniques known to have been used at the time, some assumptions may seem more realistic than others. The remaining uncertainties in this matter make it advisable not to conclude.

A discovery made in 1954, along the south face of the Great Pyramid, is of particular interest. Two boat-shaped excavations, in line with each other and covered with great standing stone slabs, contained Pharaoh's funeral barges. Only one of these pits has been opened; the other one is still sealed, maybe for reasons of conservation, maybe to allow future generations to make a wonderful discovery. The ship had been taken apart and carefully stored and has now been brought out and reassembled by the Egyptian Antiquities Organization. This splendid masterpiece has its own museum, especially built to house it. It is made up of some six hundred and fifty components totaling one thousand two hundred and twenty-four pieces of wood, mostly Lebanese cedar. At present, it measures 140 feet in length and 19 feet in width. There are neither nails nor wooden plugs: all is assembled with halfa (Spanish grass) ropes whose main quality is to swell in water and allow the ship to float.

Merneptah before Re'-Harakhty

This beautiful, multicolored relief is from the grave of Merneptah, pharaoh of the 19th dynasty and successor to Ramesses II. The king wears a rather original crown that combines several different elements: the twisted ram's horns of the sun god Amun-Re', supporting two cobras flanking the atef crown with the two tall plumes, worn by Osiris, the god of the underworld. He is moving toward a falcon-headed god crowned with a solar disc, who represents Re'-Harakhty, one of the best-known forms of the sun-god. The god is giving Pharaoh a scepter topped by two symbols, the ankh cross and the djed pillar. By this gesture he transmits to the deceased life and stability in the realm of the dead.

[Tomb 8 of Merneptah, Valley of the Kings, West Thebes, Upper Egypt.]

What king ***Khufu*** achieved remains unique. Among the pyramids built along the Valley of the Nile, the only comparable one is that of his son ***Khephren***. Paradoxically, the latter seems to dominate the former on the **Giza** plateau. There are two main reasons for this: it stands on higher ground and it has conserved part of its limestone facing at the top, making it 442 feet high, much the same as the present height of ***Khufu***'s pyramid. As to the third pyramid on the plateau, that of ***Menkaure***, it is only 200 feet high and its base is 1,150 square feet.

When the archeologist **Vyse** discovered its funerary chamber in 1837, he found the magnificent basalt sarcophagus, decorated in the "palace façade" manner, and the wooden coffin bearing the cartouches of the pharaoh. Unfortunately, the vessel carrying the sarcophagus to England, foundered somewhere along the Spanish coast and the wreck has never been found in spite of strenuous efforts to locate it.

A few hundred meters from ***Khephren***'s pyramid resides *Harmakhis*, "Horus on the Horizon," the majestic guardian of the necropolis. Turned toward the East, the sphinx of **Giza** rises out of the limestone bedrock and measures around 65 feet in height and 230 feet in length. It is thought to date from the reign of ***Khephren***, but certain details suggest that it might be older. According to tradition, an emir, exasperated by its too perfect beauty and pagan smile, mutilated its face.

The end of the pyramid period

The funerary complexes of the 5th dynasty kings have the same structure as those of their predecessors. In spite of their deteriorated state, they are among Egypt's masterpieces, but all too often overlooked. Certain sanctuaries, albeit in ruins, are magnificent both by the quality of their ornamentation and by the careful choice of the materials: basalt, granite, alabaster, limestone. The reliefs of the funerary temple of **Sahura**, buried at **Abusir**, are superb examples. The most beautiful ones, transferred to the **Cairo Museum**, show scenes relating to the King's divine birth: the goddess *Hathor* suckling him, as well as scenes from crowning and jubilee ceremonies. On the site, one can still see vestiges of great architecture (granite, basalt, limestone...): storehouses, pavements, etc.

With ***Unas***, the last king of the 5th dynasty, whose funerary complex at **Saqqara** is very well preserved, appear the first religious texts engraved on the walls of the tomb: the **"Pyramid Texts."**

"King Unas has departed to Heaven,
Heron, he has flown into the air,
He has embraced the Heavens like a falcon,
Oh, all powerful sun-god, your son is coming to you,
He commands the divine ship."

The funerary books

The Valley of the Kings is situated on the west bank of the Nile, the bank of the dead, according to the ancient Egyptians. It harbors the tombs of pharaohs from the 18th, 19th and 20th dynasties. Apart from that of Tutankhamun, they have all been looted, even in the times of the pharaohs. Nevertheless, although the funerary treasures are no longer there, the tombs still conserve the memories of magnificent burial ceremonies. Cut deeply into the rock face, the largest of these underground chambers are 300 feet long and their walls are covered with engraved or painted scenes from funerary books, exclusively reserved for members of the royalty. The "Book of the Gates" and the "Book of what there is in the realm of the Dead" are two versions of the same idea whose purpose is to identify the pharaoh with the sun-god Re'. To achieve his goal, the deceased must be familiar with this host of mysterious figures, charged with symbols, because all of them participate in the daily rebirth of the sun.

[Tomb 9 of Ramesses VI, Valley of the Kings, West Thebes, Upper Egypt.]

This is the beginning of the version reserved for ***Unas***. In fact, it is a series of spells, quite varied and totally independent of each other, intended to insure for the deceased a safe passage to the realm beyond and a life among the chosen. These magic incantations are meant to equip the deceased with whatever he needs to survive, to purify his soul and overcome obstacles. The spells and the texts have enormous power which is released by the magic of the words when they are recited during the funeral service and the magic of writing the funerary texts on the walls of the tomb. The **"Pyramid Texts"** were exclusively reserved for the king during the Old Kingdom but, over the centuries, they develop continuously, enriched by a variety of influences. They are taken up and transformed by civilians during the Middle Kingdom under the name of **"Texts of the Sarcophagi"** and, during the New Kingdom, they are the basis for the **"Book of the Dead,"** which is the most elaborate version of this type of religious writings.

Mentuhotpe, a pharaoh of the 11th dynasty, breaks with tradition and chooses to be buried at **Thebes** in Upper Egypt. He picks the rocky cirque at **Deir el-Bahri** on the west bank of the Nile, the very spot selected by queen ***Hatshepsut*** for her "Castle of Millions of Years," some five hundred years later. He builds himself a funerary complex whose structure is patterned on those of the Old Kingdom but adds various architectural elements that give the monument a unique look. From the low temple, a road leads upward in a westerly direction to a courtyard, formerly planted with trees. From there, a ramp runs up to the first terrace supported by a series of sandstone pillars. The pyramid rests on a second terrace, lined with colonnades on three sides. The funerary chamber lies to the west of the sanctuary, under the cliff. According to a report from the reign of ***Ramesses XI***, it

was still intact at that time. However, very few things have been found here: models of ships, a **naos**, staffs, scepters, etc. His cenotaph was more richly endowed. It is said that the archeologist **Howard Carter** found the entrance by chance: his horse stumbled at this particular spot, which is why it is called the "The Horse Gate." A long corridor leads to a vaulted chamber underneath the pyramid. It contained various small objects and amulets but, above all, an anonymous sarcophagus and an imposing statue of ***Mentuhotpe*** sitting down, dressed in his jubilee costume, wearing the red crown of Upper Egypt, his face painted black to emphasize his identification with Osiris, the god of the dead.

The kings of the 12th dynasty, whose tombs are located at **El Lisht**, **Dahshur** and in the region of **El Faiyum**, returned to more traditional types of constructions, modeled on those of the Old Kingdom. They still use the pyramid as a tomb but change some of its features. First, the **"Pyramid texts"** disappear: there are no inscriptions on the walls. Second, the pyramids are smaller and built of much smaller stones or even mud bricks. Finally, inside them, the arrangements of the chambers are more complex in an attempt to confuse grave robbers.

The Valley of the Kings

Tuthmosis I introduces a drastic change into the structure of the funerary complex. He separates the grave, situated in the **Valley of the Kings**, and the funerary temple, the "Castle of Millions of Years," built on the edge of the desert. On the west bank of the Nile, just below the Western Summit, lies the "Seat of *Ma'at*," the necropolis of the New-Kingdom pharaohs. It consists of two wadis: to the West, the **Valley of the Monkeys**, containing four tombs, among which is that of ***Amenhotep III***, and of the Holy Father ***Ay***; to the East, the **Valley of the Kings**, in Arabic **Biban el-Moluk**, i.e., "The Gates of the Kings," containing fifty-eight tombs from the 18th, 19th and 20th dynasties.

Some of them are just excavations filled with rubble while others still hold memories of sumptuous funeral ceremonies, although the funerary treasures are no longer there. The example of ***Tutankhamun***, if it can be considered as such, shows the wealth that accompanied Pharaoh on his journey to the beyond: chapels, sarcophagi, funeral masks, chariots, breast ornaments, weapons, dishes, clothes, caskets, staffs, furniture, etc., in addition to the special funerary goods, which were as magnificent as they were abundant: **ushebtis**, canopic jars, amulets, etc. This is surprising considering the relative insignificance of ***Tutankhamun*** in Egyptian history and makes us wonder about the treasures accompanying kings such as ***Amenhotep III*** or ***Ramesses II***.

Nephthys and Serket

Each one of the deities represented on the walls of a tomb plays a specific role in the journey of the deceased toward the realm of the dead. Some help to guide him through the meanders of the nether world, others participate in the mummification and funeral ceremonies, still others are there to protect the deceased, particularly his body or his mummified internal organs. The latter were placed in four canopic jars, stored in a small chapel and protected by the funerary goddesses: Isis, Nephthys, Serket and Neith. Here, in the tomb of Khaemwaset, buried in the Valley of the Queens, we see, on the left, the goddess Nephthys who watches over the lungs and, to the right, the scorpion-goddess Serket who watches over the intestines.

[Tomb 44 of Khaemwaset, Valley of the Queens, West Thebes, Upper Egypt.]

Following pages

Ramesses III and Shu

Having died in infancy, several of the sons of Ramesses III were buried in the Valley of the Queens. The most beautiful of these rock-cut graves is the one that belongs to Khaemwaset, where the colors have stayed wonderfully fresh. The paintings and reliefs on the walls are different from traditional ones because the dead boy appears before the funerary gods accompanied by his father, who is responsible for his child's safety as he travels through the underworld. In this scene, the king, wearing the red crown of Lower Egypt, greets the god Shu. The most astonishing aspect of this tomb is that the images are extremely naïve and their inscriptions very short: maybe because the deceased is a child.

[Tomb 44 of Khaemwaset, Valley of the Queens, West Thebes, Upper Egypt.]

Their graves, initially kept secret, *"seen by nobody, heard of by nobody,"* are said to have attracted looters very early on. The first robberies, observed during the reign of ***Ramesses IX*** in the 20th dynasty, seem to have been insignificant and, if the documents, texts and various court records and stories are to be believed, generally disregarded by high officials and inspectors responsible for the surveillance of the **West Thebes** necropolis. However, only some twenty years later, the robberies start again with renewed energy, during the reign of ***Ramesses XI***. At this time, the graves are carefully inspected in order to save anything that has escaped the looters. Damaged mummies are restored and it is finally decided to put all of them into two hiding places: partly in the grave of ***Amenhotep II*** and partly in a secret chamber cut into the cliff near **Deir el-Bahri** (the royal mummies of ***Amenhotep I***, ***Tuthmosis III***, ***Sethos I***, ***Ramesses II***, and others).

It is not until the 19th century that the problems of grave robbery surface again. Beginning in 1876, objects stamped with royal and prestigious cartouches appear on the antiquities markets, which suggests the existence of a considerable but unknown supply source. After a lengthy search, the French archeologist **Maspéro** finally solves the mystery: Ahmed Abd el-Rassul, living in **Gurnah**, a small village on the west bank of **Thebes**, is selling off, little by little, the hidden royal treasures. In 1881 the mummies and their remaining riches leave **Luxor** for the **Cairo Museum**: *"From Luxor to Qift, on both banks of the Nile, wild-haired peasant women ran beside the boat screaming and the men fired shots in the air as they do at funerals."* When the boat arrives in **Cairo**, the captain declares the cargo in order to pay the required unloading taxes, but the amazed official in charge does not know what tariff to use and finally registers the cargo as… dried fish!

The general arrangements of all the graves are fairly similar: a door cut vertically into the rock, a long, progressively narrowing, corridor with lateral wall niches or chapels and one or several funeral chambers. The tombs are always over 300 feet long. The eye of the visitor is immediately attracted by the decorations engraved or painted on the walls: hundreds of figures, crowded together, flow from one end to the other of the funerary chambers. Pictures telling the story of the lives and the funerary ceremonies of the dead kings decorate the walls of their "Castle of Millions of Years," the name often given to the funerary temples of **West Thebes**. But the images relating to the journey of the royal soul in the nether world are reserved for the tombs. These tales, told partially or entirely in pictures, are collected in funerary books of more or less ancient origin.

The **"Litanies of the Sun"** describe the sun-god, Re': his qualities, functions, attributes, nature, transformations, seventy-five in number, that the sovereign must know in order to be able to identify himself with the god. The **"Book of the Opening of the Mouth"** details the rites that will give the mummy and the statue of the Double the power to receive offerings and be nourished by them. The **"Book of What There is in the Netherworld"** and the **"Book of the Gates"** are two versions of the same idea: the identification of the king with Re'. The other world is divided into twelve regions watered by the nether Nile whose banks are populated by strange spirits symbolizing all the ills that the body can suffer from; this is why reptiles are shown as armed with picks or knives. On the river floats the solar barge carrying the god Re' and other divinities: the jackal *Apuaïu* guide of the nether roads; *Horus* the herald, *Hathor* the patron goddess of the crew, the Double of the god *Shu*; *Hu* the crew; *Sa* the pilot; the guard; the captain. For a given region, the text announces the name of the region, the name of the Hour of the Night that lives there, the name of its guardian, the real extent of his territory, the names of the spirits found there, the words pronounced by the dead Sun when he enters the region: those who know all these names and all these words can be united with the Sun.

The tomb of Tutankhamun

Tutankhamun. The very name fascinates and today we are forced to admit that, by himself, he symbolizes all of pharaonic Egypt. Nevertheless, nothing predestined this young man to such a prestigious fate. A ruler without any great influence, a sickly boy with a weak constitution, ***Tutankhamun*** dies at the age of nineteen in what seems to have been an atmosphere of general indifference: he had reigned for only a couple of years at a time when the country was slowly recovering from the troubled reign of ***Amenhotep IV-Akhenaten***. In fact, his fame stems from the discovery of his undisturbed tomb by **Howard Carter**.

The goddess Neith

The Valley of the Queens contains the graves of the royal wives and princesses as well as certain royal princes of the New Kingdom. Around eighty rock-cut graves have been uncovered. Some of them have been identified with certainty, others, like this one, are still anonymous because the names of the owners have been chipped away in subsequent periods. Two baboons are seated in a tabernacle in a traditional pose: as the baboon is a solar symbol, these two are looking at the morning sun. In front of the tabernacle stands the goddess Neith, crowned by her emblem, which is said to represent two bows tied together in their case. In the afterlife, she watches over the internal organs of the deceased together with Isis, Nephthys and Serket.
[Anonymous tomb,
Valley of the Queens,
West Thebes, Upper Egypt.]

Tutankhamun was not found in his original grave. His premature death obliges the high officials of the necropolis to abandon the work on his own tomb, situated at the extreme western end of the **Valley of the Kings**, and bury the young king at a site initially prepared for the Holy Father, ***Ay***, his immediate successor. For several years, **Carter**, Chief of **Lord Carnarvon**'s private mission, already suspected that this tomb existed. A few amulets and various other objects, engraved with the royal name of ***Tutankhamun*** encouraged the British archeologist to explore the area between the tombs of ***Ramesses VI*** and ***Ramesses IX***, but without really believing that he would be successful.

Finally, on November 4, 1922, he uncovers, first, one step cut into the rock, then, a second and a third **Carter** had found the tomb of ***Tutankhamun***. He immediately sends a telegram to his associate, **Lord Carnarvon**, worded as follows: *"Have finally made an extraordinary discovery in the Valley: a magnificent tomb whose seals are intact; have closed it again to await your arrival; congratulutions."*

However, he does not yet know if this is indeed the tomb of the young ***Tutankhamun***. A few days later his hopes become reality: *"I have **Tutankhamun** and I believe it to be... intact."* Subsequently, **Carter** wrote these words: *"Euphoria had taken hold of us without leaving us one moment for reflection, but for the first time we became conscious of our responsibilities and the prodigious task in front of us. This was no ordinary discovery which could be processed in the space of a season; there was no precedent to show us how to proceed. The undertaking exceeded the scope of all past experience, bewildered us and, at least at that moment, seemed overwhelming compared to all human action, whatever it might be."*

In fact, like all the rock-cut tombs in the **Valley of the Kings**, that of ***Tutankhamun*** had already been violated during the 20th dynasty. Fortunately, a necropolis official had noticed the night-time incursions and had rapidly put a stop to them. After having inventoried the tomb, he had closed it and put his own seals on the entrances. At this time, the excavations start on the tomb of ***Ramesses VI***, its immediate neighbor. Through negligence, the excavated rubble is not removed but deposited in front of ***Tutankhamun***'s grave and, with time, hides it completely. This is how a tomb, still filled with all its treasures, fell into total oblivion.

The tomb presents very little interest. It is small and consists of four rooms of which only the funerary chamber is decorated. The steps lead to a long slightly sloping corridor at the end of which lies the first chamber, the **Antechamber**, giving access, on the left, to a small storeroom, the **Annex**, and, to the right, to the **Funerary Chamber**, which leads into another room, the **Treasury**. All these rooms were filled to overflowing with all kinds of objects, heaped on top of each other in total disorder. It is, in fact, difficult to imagine how this wealth of objects, now exhibited in the **Cairo Museum**, could fit into the four rooms. The processing of all the precious objects actually lasted for ten years, during which time **Carter** and his team worked assiduously, inventorying, counting, restoring, drawing, photographing, bringing them out and transferring them. There are hundreds of amulets, pieces of tableware, **ushebtis**, weapons, staves, scepters or officers' wands, stools, thrones, beds, chests or low tables, statuettes of gods, funerary barges, jewelry, ornaments, bracelets, brooches or pectorals: all made of gold, silver, electrum, precious or semiprecious stones, glass paste, alabaster, gilded wood, ebony, and so on.

Finally the long awaited moment arrives: **Carter** announces that the work in the antechamber is finished and that the opening of the funerary chamber is imminent. This is February 17, 1923. **Lord Carnarvon**'s brother describes the scene: *"Rows of chairs had been placed in the first chamber of the tomb, completely empty except for the two statuettes of the king, at one end. They flanked the sealed door, below which a small wooden podium hid the hole through which they had entered the first time. Poor old Porch (**Carnarvon**) was as nervous as a schoolboy caught misbehaving; he was afraid that it would be discovered that there was already a hole. He was also, and what is more natural, very excited. Although he had a very good idea of what was in there, he certainly could not help thinking that he was living one of the great moments that very few people ever experience... He started by making a very beautiful speech, concise and to the point, the main thrust of which was to thank everybody. Then it was Carter's turn to make a speech, not a very good one, because he was nervous and expressed himself with difficulty; he talked about science and the dangers threatening the recovered objects."*

As for **Carter**, he explains: "... *When, after ten minutes, I had made a sufficiently big hole, I shone an electric torch through it. The light revealed an amazing spectacle: there, less than a meter from the door, as far as the eye could see, blocking the passage, stretched a wall that seemed to be made of solid gold... Without a doubt, we were in the funerary chamber: what rose above us was indeed one of the great gilded chapels where kings are laid to rest. This construction was so vast... that, except for a small space, it filled the whole chamber and was separated from the four walls only by a space fifty centimeters wide, while its roof, decorated by a torus molding, almost reached the ceiling....*"

Four gold-plated wooden chapels, fitting inside each other, sheltered a quartzite sarcophagus engraved with funerary scenes. Inside, three coffins of decreasing size held the body of the dead king. The two outer coffins were built of gilded wood, inlaid with multicolored-glass paste and semiprecious stones. The interior coffin was made of solid gold, decorated with fine enamels and inlaid with semiprecious stones and weighed 110 kilos. All three of them represent ***Tutankhamun*** in the attitude of *Osiris* with the **heka** cross and the flail crossed on his chest. The face, enclosed in a **nemes**, wore the divine false beard and the emblems of Upper and Lower Egypt, the cobra-goddess *Wadjit* and the vulture-goddess, *Nekhbet*. Finally, the mummified king appeared, his head covered by a funerary mask and a headdress, his body decorated with jewelry and pectorals, his extremities encased in finger stalls, all made of solid gold. When the strips of cloth were unwound from the mummy, nearly one hundred and fifty amulets were discovered, carved from various precious materials and placed on the body to protect it.

In the **Treasury** chamber were assembled the precious objects that had been used in the funerary cult: jewelry caskets, small naos containing statuettes of ***Tutankhamun***, funerary barges, statues of divinities and, in particular, the casket of canopic jars containing the internal organs of the deceased. It looked like a large tabernacle of gilded wood placed on a sled. On its four sides, *Isis*, *Nephthys*, *Neith* and *Serket* protected the casket with outstretched arms and their heads turned to one side. It sheltered another smaller, alabaster casket with, in the corners, relief carvings of the same four funerary goddesses. Inside, were the four alabaster canopic jars, closed by a lid in the image of the king. Each one contained a small gold sarcophagus, around thirty centimeters long, holding the mummified internal organs of ***Tutankhamun***.

The **Antechamber** and the **Annex** harbored a diverse and disordered collection of objects that were probably not in their place of origin. In the Annex, everything was thrown together, broken, ripped open, overturned. The material had doubtlessly been moved by robbers, because we know that the tomb had been violated in the early Ramesside era. However, nobody knows why the necropolis officials had not deemed it necessary to put the things in order in this room, although they had conscientiously done so in the other rooms of the tomb. Beds, caskets, dismantled chariots, stools, folding chairs, small thrones, low tables and vases made up the funerary furnishings. There were also great numbers of scepters, fly whisks, musical instruments, bows, staffs, headrests, clothes, jewelry, ornaments, etc. Most of them were made of precious metals, gilded wood or alabaster inlaid with ivory, lapis lazuli or turquoise.

The Valley of the Queens

It used to be called the "Place of Beauty". Today, the southernmost wadi of the Theban necropolis bears the name **Biban el-Harim**, the "Gates of the Queens" and, more commonly, the **Valley of the Queens**. In this valley lie the tombs of the royal wives and princesses from the Ramesside era, as well as those of the sons of ***Ramesses III***, who died in childhood. To this day, around eighty tombs have been discovered, but the systematic investigations are not yet finished and it is entirely possible that on-going explorations might reveal the existence of unknown rock-cut tombs.

Clearly, all these tombs are not of equal interest: some of them are simply indeterminate excavations, either without inscriptions or unfinished or terribly deteriorated by the humidity in the soil or by deliberate burning. Others figure among the masterpieces of ancient Egypt because their carvings and paintings are remarkably well preserved. Of all these tombs, the most out-standing one is, without a doubt, that belonging to the wife of ***Rameses II***, queen ***Nefertari***.

For many years, continuous water infiltration and ground movement have been threatening the paintings inside the tomb. Called on by the Egyptian Antiquities Organization, foreign specialists have therefore completely restored and insulated the tomb, which has been closed to the public for a considerable time. On the walls, ***Nefertari***, wearing a long dress of translucent linen and the crown of the goddess *Mut*, is depicted worshipping the Egyptian divinities: *Osiris*, *Horus*, *Harakhty*, *Isis*, *Nephthys*, *Hathor*, *Ma'at*, *Ptah*, etc. These paintings, which are exceptionally graceful and have a beautifully fresh coloring, are remarkable for their careful and skilled workmanship.

Two other tombs deserve special attention: those of the royal children ***Amenherkhopshef*** and ***Khaemwaset***, two sons of ***Ramesses III*** who died in childhood. In both of them the reliefs, painted in bright and lively colors, are exceptionally well preserved. Here, Pharaoh himself ushers his children into the presence of the spirits, guardians of the nether and subterranean regions. He also introduces them to the funerary deities and to the protectors of the canopic jars, the **four sons of Horus**: *Imset*, *Hapy*, *Qebehsenuf* and *Duamutef*. On the walls of the adjoining halls and in the corridors, there are several extracts from the **"Book of the Gates,"** naïvely illustrated because of the youth of the occupants.

The tomb of Ramesses VI

The most interesting feature of the tomb of Ramesses VI are the blue and yellow-figured astronomical representations on the ceilings of the halls. They describe the journey of the sun through the night and the day, both divided into twelve hours. The king accompanies the sun's ship and its crew on their journey and participates in the labors of the gods as they struggle with the evil spirits and the great serpent Apophis. Hieroglyphic texts at the beginning of the scenes indicate in what hour they are, the names of those who live there, the spells that must be recited when one meets them, etc.
[Tomb 9 of Ramesses VI, Valley of the Kings, West Thebes, Upper Egypt.]

The Royal Tombs at Tanis

The tombs discovered in 1939 by **Pierre Monet**, at **Tanis**, south of the Temple of *Amun*, belong to the kings and high officials of the 21st and 22nd dynasties and are of a particular type that emerged during the Low Period: that of the "tomb in the temple courtyard." The six known tombs are underground and, to a great extent, built with recovered limestone blocks, although some of them have antechambers, annexes and funerary chambers enclosed by granite blocks. Others have a well in front of the grave or consist of only one chamber. The first two were used as family graves. Thus, the one destined for ***Psusennes I*** was built to accommodate not only the king but also his wife ***Mutnedjemet*** and the high official **Wundebaunded**. The king's son **Ankhefenmut** reposed in a side chamber of the tomb; later, they were joined by pharaohs ***Amenemope*** and ***Sheshonq II***, the latter was put in the antechamber in a superb silver coffin with a falcon's head. In the tomb of ***Osorkon II***, his eldest son, the Grand Priest of *Amun*, ***Hornakht*** was laid to rest behind his father's sarcophagus and, in a side chamber, ***Takelot II***. In the tomb of ***Sheshonq III***, vestiges were found of funerary materials belonging to ***Sheshonq I***, whose grave remains undiscovered to this day. In short, so many questions remain unanswered that there is no way of determining with precision how this necropolis was laid out.

The walls of the funerary chambers are decorated with scenes representing the journey of the sovereign in the beyond and inscriptions invoking *Ptah-Sokaris*, the sun-god Re'-*Harakhty*, *Osiris*, the Theban triad or even

Aten, principal personification of the solar disc. However, all these pictures give only a very fragmented summary of the traditional royal funerary books, as seen in the **Valley of the Kings**, no doubt owing to lack of space, since the tombs are small, but also to the fact that the beliefs concerning life after death were constantly changing.

The tomb of ***Psusennes I*** was untouched: it had totally escaped the grave robbers. Three sarcophagi, one inside the other, contained the body of the king: the first one, of red granite, belonged to ***Merneptah***; the second one, of black granite, was that of an official of the 19th dynasty; the third one, of silver, showed the king as *Osiris*. The grave of ***Amenemope*** also contained a beautiful funerary collection, in particular, a solid-gold mask, rather remarkable because of the sweetness of the facial expression. Of the mummies, however, there remained nothing but bones. The furnishings, among them the vases, as well as the silver, gold and bronze ornaments, were inscribed with dedications from members of the royal family or from local dignitaries, but also from Theban priests of *Amun*. This proves that, in spite of the separation of powers between Upper and Lower Egypt, there was still a certain friendliness in the relations between **Tanis** in the North and **Thebes** in the South.

THE TEMPLES, DIVINE DWELLINGS

Cult temples and funerary temples

The screened windows of the temple at Karnak

The great temple at Karnak, dedicated to Amun, the god of the Kingdom, is the most colossal architectural complex ever built in Egypt. It is laid out along two axes and has ten pylons, as well as chapels, courtyards, storage spaces and warehouses in great numbers, all of them assembled in a vast space surrounded by a wall. It is, in fact, the result of a series of successive modifications because, during nearly two thousand years, from the Middle Kingdom to the Greco-Roman period, the sovereigns kept enlarging the sanctuary and enhancing its beauty. This is the large pillared, or hypostyle, hall between pylons 2 and 3 that were constructed during the 18th and 19th dynasties. It has twelve central columns, over 75 feet high, and one hundred and twenty-two lateral columns, one third shorter than the others. The difference in height is compensated by a subtle system of clearstories, pierced stone trellises with closely-spaced bars, that allow diffuse light to enter the hall.

[Temple of Amun, Karnak, East Thebes, Upper Egypt.]

To begin with, the temples devoted to the gods and the funerary temples were two quite distinct structures that must not, under any circumstances, be confused with each other. The divine temple is the "house of the god," the very place where the creation is sustained due to the ceaseless activity of the gods. As opposed to this, the role of the funerary temple is to allow the deceased to survive by means of rituals and offerings. During the New Kingdom, these two entities were merged without actually becoming one and the same: the "Castles of Millions of Years," funerary temples of the 18th, 19th and 20th dynasties, are built with the intention of joining the superhuman destiny of Pharaoh to that of the gods and, in particular, to the spirit of *Amun*. Therefore, what is more natural than to build monuments whose structure and decorations resemble those of the temple of *Amun* himself?

Organization of the cult temples

In Egypt, temples dedicated to the gods date back to very ancient times, as shown by the numerous foundations of religious buildings found along the Nile Valley. Unfortunately, the few vestiges from the Old and Middle Kingdoms do not provide sufficient information allowing us to determine what the temples really looked like in this distant past. One of the reasons for this is that the mud bricks, extensively used in these constructions, have not always withstood the test of time; another reason is that blocks of nobler materials such as limestone and granite were often systematically reutilized in later constructions. Only the solar temple at **Abu Gorab**, from the 5th dynasty, and the kiosk of ***Senusret I*** at **Karnak** still remain. However, the cult complexes built from the New Kingdom until the end of the Roman era give us quite a precise idea of the organization of the religious buildings. There are many examples: although the structures are sometimes very dissimilar, the idea behind them is always more or less the same. Inside a small chapel there is a stone tabernacle, the **naos**, which contains the image of the god and his portable barge in which the divine statue rides around on days of processions and feasts. This chapel is surrounded by a great number of halls devoted to the cult of secondary gods invited for a certain period into the temple compound. Lateral chambers are used as sacristies or to store fabrics, jewelry and objects required for the cult. Opening out from this core and becoming increasingly vast and luminous farther away from the sanctuary, there is a succession of rooms, varying in number according to the size of the temple, the outer ones being hypostyle halls whose roofs are supported by columns. These halls eventually lead to a courtyard furnished with statues and altars, even small shrines. The pylon, the monumental entrance, flanked by two high, massive stone piles gives access to the courtyard. Additional structures are dotted around: the **sacred lake**, the House of life, the well, living quarters for the religious staff and the storehouses of the temple. A brick wall with several doors encloses the compound, which is reached by a wide avenue bordered by sphinxes, the **dromos**.

The traditional cult of a god follows the rythm of human life. At dawn, after having purified themselves, the priests open the temple and prepare the food for the god. Then comes the ceremony of the "awakening of the god." The Grand Priest opens the sealed **naos**, while reciting the chants and the words of the morning. The meal of meat, bread, vegetables and fruit, beer and wine is placed before the god. The priests then withdraw to let the god "eat his breakfast." When the invisible matter of these foods has

been absorbed by the god, the offerings are laid on the altars of the secondary divinities. Afterwards, they are brought to the workshops to be shared and eaten by the priests. After the meal, it is time for the grooming: the statue is washed, dressed in new clothes and ornaments and scented. A weaver's workshop, inside the temple compound, is devoted to making the god's linen clothing, which is kept in the "hall of fabrics" next to the sanctuary. Finally, the Grand Priest closes the **naos** while pronouncing the ritual words: *"May no evil being penetrate into this sanctuar.y."* At midday, the service is much simpler and consists in sprinkling water and burning incense, but no meal is served. In the evening ritual, at sundown, the ceremonies of the morning are repeated and when the statue has been replaced in the **naos**, the latter is locked and sealed until the next morning. On feast days, the ceremonies are more complex and more solemn, often including a short journey by the statue of the god on the **sacred lake** in the divine barge.

The temple of Amun at Karnak

The arrival of the 18th dynasty is marked by an increased importance of the god *Amun-Re'*. He was already god of **Thebes** when this city was no more than a humble village. However, from the Middle Kingdom onward, his power and influence grow. When **Thebes** is chosen as the official capital of the New Kingdom, he becomes a national and dynastic divinity, a universal and creator god. The theologians associate him in a triad with the goddess *Mut* and the child-god *Khons*. Throughout the period of the New Kingdom, until the end of the Greco-Roman era, temples are built for them all over the country but none is comparable to that at **Karnak** or even **Luxor**.

The rise of **Thebes** helps to increase the wealth and influence of the cult of *Amun*, which reaches such proportions that the great temple at **Karnak** becomes a national sanctuary continually receiving donations from the pharaohs. Its clergy comes to wield considerable power

and, very rapidly, its head, the Grand Priest, attains a position as important as that of the highest officials in the country: he manages the vast estates of the god which are not subjected to the authority of the king. The foreign conquests bring Egypt enormous wealth in the form of booty carried back by the victorious armies and tributes extracted from the conquered countries. The greater part of these riches is offered to *Amun* as thanksgiving offerings and his temples turn into powerful economic centers. As opposed to other temples, the great temple at **Karnak** does not have a uniform plan because, for over two thousand years, from the Middle Kingdom to the Greco-Roman period, it was constantly being modified. It is, in fact, a collection of different buildings that have grown up in the course of the centuries. The layout of this great cult center is therefore rather complex. It is made up of three main groups of buildings, each surrounded by a wall: the temple of *Montu*, the temple of *Amun* and the temple of *Mut* which is linked to that of *Amun* by a **dromos**.

The growth of **Karnak** is quite logical: around the initial 12th dynasty sanctuary, all sorts of buildings, courtyards and pylons were added as the temple was extended and each sovereign built his contribution in front of that of his predecessor. The entrance to the temple is therefore through the most recent additions and one gradually goes back in time until one arrives at the Middle Kingdom sanctuary.

The temple of *Amun* has two great axes: an east-west one with six pylons, numbered from 1 to 6, and a north-south one with four pylons, numbered 7 to 10. This numbering, although necessary, is fictitious and does not take account of the chronology; it just follows the route along which visitors are guided. For example, from east to west, pylon 1 is the most recent, pylon 6 is the most ancient. Apart from the major elements of the temple of *Amun*, the principal constructions inside the wall are: a temple dedicated to the child-god *Khons* and a **sacred lake** where the god can enjoy an outing in his ship.

Wadi el-Sebua

Today, this temple stands on the sandy banks of Lake Nasser but this is not its original site because it is one of the Nubian temples moved, with the help of UNESCO, when the Great Aswan Dam was built. In Arabic, Wadi el-Sebua means the "Valley of the Lions," which refers to the avenue of sphinxes, wearing the crown of Upper and Lower Egypt, which leads to the entrance of the temple. This building, dedicated to the two sun-gods Amun-Re' and Re'-Harakhty, dates from the reign of Ramesses II and although it is situated in Nubian territory, around 85 miles south of Aswan, it is an expression of the purest pharaonic tradition.
[Temple of Ramesses II, Wadi el-Sebua, Nubia]

Pylon 1 gives access to a wide courtyard with various, totally independent, cult complexes: in the center stand the ruins of a gigantic kiosk, erected by ***Taharqo***, of the 25th dynasty; to one side, there is a boat repository by ***Sethos II*** and a sanctuary by ***Ramesses III***, both of which became part of the temple when the courtyard was built. At one end, we see pylon 2, destroyed by an earthquake in the first centuries of our era. It was built of stones from eleven different buildings, among others a few thousand **"talatates,"** rough blocks used in the constructions by ***Akhenaten***.

One then enters the great hypostyle hall which offers one of the most amazing sights one could possibly see: it is 330 feet wide and 172 feet long and contains one

hundred and thirty-four monumental columns. The twelve central ones have papyrus-shaped capitals and support a 35 feet high ceiling. The one hundred and twenty-two remaining columns are a third shorter, and the height in the center forms a **clearstory** that lets the light filter through. This hall was built in several stages. The twelve central columns date back to the reign of ***Amenhotep III***; the side columns and pylon 2 are attributed to ***Horemheb***. The decorations were begun by ***Ramesses I***, continued by ***Sethos I*** and ***Ramesses II*** and completed by ***Ramesses IV***. The scenes show the king before the divinities of the Egyptian pantheon, participating in processions and cult ceremonies.

Pylon 3, built under ***Amenhotep III***, closes the great hypostyle hall. The filling inside the great piles has yielded around one thousand three hundred stone blocks belonging to thirteen different buildings, among them the kiosk by ***Senusret I*** and the alabaster repository by ***Amenhotep I***, today exhibited in the open-air museum at **Karnak**. Then comes a succession of vestibules and pylons, all very damaged. At the heart of this series of buildings, stands one of the two obelisks set up by queen ***Hatshepsut*** on the occasion of her jubilee. It is over 95 feet high and is considered one of the most beautiful in Egypt. Tradition has it that, barely ascended to the throne, ***Tuthmosis III*** had a wooden or mortar casing built around the two obelisks so as not to have to look at them. This may be the secret of their excellent state of preservation.

Pylon 6 gives access to a courtyard leading to a granite hall, erroneously called **"Sanctuary of Philip Arrhidaeus,"** which was used as a ship repository. Of the **"holy of holies,"** the most important part of the temple, there is nothing left, no masonry or even foundations. Nowadays, one therefore crosses an almost empty space to reach the last collection of buildings, dating from the era of ***Tuthmosis III***. The **"Banquet Hall," "Akh Menu"** to the Egyptians, is situated at the very end of the east-west axis, and its numerous annexes form a separate entity, still in a good state of preservation. The access is through a hypostyle hall, whose roof is still intact, surrounded by pillars and containing two rows of columns. The ritual scenes on the walls may not always be very original but the quality of the painting is outstanding and, despite the ravages caused by the transformation of this space into a church in the 6th century, the reliefs still show beautiful traces of color. At the end, doors cut into the masonry lead to halls, annexes and storerooms. The famous **"Chamber of the Ancestors,"** which is now in the **Louvre Museum**, comes from this site and shows ***Tuthmosis III*** making offerings before fifty-seven kings, thought to be his predecessors.

The island of Philae

Built in the Greco-Roman period on an island near Aswan, the sanctuary of Philae contains several buildings among which the most famous is dedicated to the goddess Isis, wife of Osiris. Her cult was one of the most popular in all Egypt and long resisted the influence of Christianity. It is said that the sanctuary of Philae was still in activity when the doors of all the others in the Nile Valley had been closed for many years. In fact, it was the Roman emperor Justinian who, in 551, definitely closed the temple of Isis. Thus, after having lasted for nearly three thousand five hundred years, the pharaonic civilization fell into oblivion together with its means of expression, the hieroglyphic script.

[Temple of Isis and its annexes, Philae, Upper Egypt.]

The north-south axis intersects the east-west one at pylons 3 and 4. Four pylons, separated by courtyards and formerly joined by walls, succeed each other on the way to the temple of Mut. In front of pylon 7, said to have been rebuilt by ***Tuthmosis III***, is the so-called **"Hidden-treasure courtyard,"** which gets its name from the surprising discovery, under its paving stones, of a great number of objects: almost eight hundred stone statues, a thousand seven hundred bronze statuettes and several thousand ex-votos which are all on display in the **Cairo Museum**.

The temple at Luxor

Among all the official ceremonies honoring the Theban triad, the **Feast of the New Year** or **Feast of Opet** was the most fabulous, because it prompted the construction of a special temple. In the Theban religion, this special cult site is the temple of **Luxor**, in the rest of the country it is called the temple of **Amun of Opet**. The ceremony took place in the second month of the flood. The divine triad was transported in barges up the Nile from **Karnak** to **Luxor**. In the midst of a rejoicing crowd, twenty-four priests carried *Mut* and *Khons* to their respective barges while thirty porters brought *Amun*. Pharaoh embarked in the barge transporting the principal god. Men towed the barges to their landing place, surrounded by milling crowds who chanted prayers until the whole procession had arrived at its destination. The gods stayed ten days at **Luxor** and for their return journey the same ceremonies were repeated.

In order to measure the importance of he cult of *Amun* during the New Kingdom, one simply has to examine the **Luxor** temple, which was built to be used for only ten days each year. It is situated on the east bank of the river and was originally called **"the Southern Residence,"** because of the ceremonies of the **Feast of Opet** that took place there every year. It seems to have been in use for over a thousand years until it was eventually turned into a Roman camp which gave it its present name of **Luxor**: **el-Qasr** means "camp" or "castle" in Arabic. As opposed to **Karnak**, which was constantly being transformed, **Luxor** is mainly the work of only two sovereigns: ***Amenhotep III*** and ***Ramesses II*** although, at one time or another, certain other pharaohs have inscribed their cartouches and added some less important decorative elements.

The initial layout is fairly traditional: originally, the chief architect, **Amenhotep son of Hapu**, planned a sanctuary and a hypostyle, or columned, hall, to which one gained entrance through a monumental gate in the north wall. Then he adds a courtyard surrounded by a colonnade and preceded by a pylon. In front of this complex, he constructs a double row of seven columns closed by a second pylon, and moves the entrance east. ***Tutankhamun*** continues the work on the **Luxor** site but his premature

Kom Ombo

30 miles north of Aswan stands the small temple of Kom Ombo whose unusual shape is the result of its religious vocation. It was built to honor two very different deities: Haroeris, "Horus the Great," sun and warrior-god responsible for exterminating the enemies of Re' and Sobek, the crocodile-god who protects men from the hostile powers inhabiting the marshes. Only the entrance and the first courtyard are shared by the two cults. The spaces and passages leading to the "holy of holies" are double and follow two parallel axes: the northern part is dedicated to Haroeris and the southern one to Sobek. As we see it today, the sanctuary dates back to the Greco-Roman period but, in the usual way, it has replaced a more ancient structure, probably from the New Kingdom and smaller in size.

[Temple of Sobek and Haroeris, Kom Ombo, Upper Egypt.]

death prevents him from completing the decoration of the colonnade which had been left unfinished by his predecessor. Not until the arrival of ***Ramesses II*** do new transformations appear. In front of the line of columns, he adds a new colonnaded courtyard, slightly turned to the east because of the course of the Nile, and preceded by a high pylon, which itself is preceded by six colossal statues and a pair of obelisks, 175 and 181 feet high. Both were given to France in 1831 by **Mehemet Ali**, who made this generous gesture to honor **Champollion** for having solved the mystery of the hieroglyphs. Only the smaller, western, obelisk was transported to **Paris** by the engineer **Lebas** and raised on the Place de la Concorde in 1836. In 1980, France definitively gave up all claims to the second one.

The temple at Tanis

After having seen the temples at **Karnak** and **Luxor**, it is painful to visit **Tanis**, where the experience is totally different. Everything is in ruins, jumbled stone blocks, tumbled-down columns and obelisks, toppled down a long time ago. In fact, the reputation of **Tanis** rests on the discovery, in 1939, of the royal necropolis and its rich funerary furnishings.

The city of **Tanis**, called **Zo'an** in the Bible, is situated in the north-eastern part of the Delta. Its history begins with the 21st dynasty and continues until the Roman era. The Third Intermediate Period is marked by a division of power: Upper Egypt is governed by the Grand Priests of *Amun* and Lower Egypt by the pharaohs who install their capital at **Tanis**, or **Djanet** to the ancient Egyptians. This is where ***Psusennes I*** and his successors undertake the construction of a temple in honor of the Theban triad: *Amun*, *Mut* and *Khons*. The city of **Tanis** was rediscovered in the 19th century by **Flinders Petrie** and thought to be linked to the Hyksos capital, **Avaris**, and to **Pi-Ramesses**, the Ramesside capital, because of the great number of stones from these two sites found at **Tanis**. It is indeed very difficult to interpret the history of the city.

On the site, the only remaining vestiges are granite blocks from the Hyksos or Ramesside era: they are the foundations of the sanctuary built by the kings of the 21st dynasty, who did not hesitate to recover the materials they needed from **Avaris** and **Pi-Ramesses**, situated only some twelve miles away. However, the temple itself was built of limestone on top of these foundations. Unfortunately, almost nothing remains of it because of the systematic destruction by lime-burners of

any limestone fragments available on the site. We are therefore faced with a sanctuary from the Third Intermediate Period of which only the foundations remain, and these foundations consist of recycled materials inscribed with the name ***Ramesses II***: the confusion with **Pi-Ramesses** could hardly be avoided.

There is very little left from the reign of ***Psusennes I***, except for the enormous wall of mud brick, that surrounded the site, and the core of the great temple of *Amun*. The monumental gate and most of the sanctuary date back to the 22nd dynasty, but it is very difficult to find any trace of them today. In fact, the work by the kings of the 30th dynasty and by the *Ptolemies* has erased the memory of the founders, since all of them totally remodeled the site, either by adding new sanctuaries or by transforming the existing buildings to adapt them to new beliefs.

The ptolemaic temples

No Egyptian temple is as well preserved as the one at **Edfu**, dedicated to *Horus*. It is almost intact and looks as if it had been built quite recently. This is why the study of this archetypal Egyptian temple is extremely rewarding: it reveals both what the architecture of an Egyptian temple was like and what religious decorations were engraved on its walls. However, it seems scarcely possible to consider this building as an absolute example, because one must keep in mind that it was built by the Ptolemies and, therefore, comparatively late. It is clear that temple building must have evolved a great deal since the 18th dynasty. By its size, it is one of most imposing religious centers in the Valley of the Nile: Its pylons are 117 feet high, it is 256 feet wide and 445 feet long. However, its main feature is the harmony of its layout: it was built between 237 and 57 B.C., in one continuous stretch, which is very rare.

The ptolemaic temples have some special features which probably did not exist in the preceding periods but were introduced by the Greek kings. The basic plan is completely clear. Access to the temple is through a pylon leading to a courtyard surrounded by a colonnade. Then comes a succession of hypostyle halls and vestibules through which one arrives at the sanctuary surrounded by chapels. All this is enclosed by a sandstone wall that closely encircles the temple, leaving only a narrow passage in-between. The plan is organized in such a way that the **naos**, where the statue of the god is kept, is the most central, narrowest hall with the lowest ceiling and the highest floor, making it the darkest room in the temple. The architecture is loaded with unnecessary and superfluous elements that increase the bulk of the buildings: composite capitals, large architraves, etc. The decorations show scenes taken from traditional royal iconography but, in addition, there are numerous pictures relating to cosmogonies and simple cult practices, from the daily services to more solemn ceremonies. The Greek era differs from preceding ones in that there is a new arrangement of the reliefs and the texts on the walls: henceforth, the registers, clear and straight, are set in ordered and subdivided columns. The figures acquire a different outline: instead of being flat, as formerly, they are unusually rounded, the clothing and headdresses have patterns that are no longer symbolic but ornamental, taken from religious and funerary imagery.

The temple at Edfu

It is one of the most beautiful monuments along the Nile Valley. Because it is so well preserved, this temple gives us an insight into the structure of traditional religious sites in the Ptolemaic period. Its construction, started in 237 B.C. in the reign of Ptolemy III, was finished some eighty years later, precisely, in 57 B.C. on December 5th, if we are to believe the dedication inscribed on one of the walls. On the monumental pylon giving access to the sanctuary, Ptolemy XII is depicted in the act of smiting a handful of enemies with his club as he offers them to the falcon-god Horus. Above this scene, Pharaoh is shown making offering to the divinities of the kingdom seated in an orderly row, one behind the other.
[Temple of Horus, Edfu, Upper Egypt.]

Following pages
The Pylon at Philae

All temple entrances are marked by a monumental gate, called pylon, consisting of two high trapezoidal piles flanking a low opening. The axis of the buildings is calculated in such a manner that the morning sun first strikes the space between the stone piles. This arrangement is intended to remind the people, every day, of the fundamental event in the creation of the world when, in the beginning, the sun-god emerged from chaos, Nun, to settle on a hillock, the primordial hill. Generally, the decorations on the pylons show Pharaoh in the process of slaughtering captives in front of the gods. The pylon of the temple of Isis conforms to this rule: here, the hero-king is Ptolemy XII and the divinities before him are Isis, Hathor and Horus.
[Temple of Isis, Philae, Upper Egypt.]

Role of the funerary temples

Every tomb contains a chapel where the rites essential to the survival of the deceased are carried out. However, it stands to reason that private and royal funerary temples are the same in name only: the former are small chapels but the latter are great temples worthy of the dignified status of their occupants. In the beginning, when the pharaohs were buried in pyramids, the funerary temples are small annexes abutting on the tomb of the king. This assumption is strengthened by the fact that there is very little information about them, because very few have survived. However, their function is quite specific: litanies and rituals are recited there, offerings and gifts for the survival of the king are deposited in the chapel. Starting with the New Kingdom, Pharaoh's tomb is cut into the Libyan rock face, on the site called the **"Valley of the Kings,"** and, at the edge of the desert west of **Thebes**, he builds a magnificent temple for himself flanked by residences and surrounded by vast estates. It is thought that these buildings are funerary complexes intended for the service of the royal tombs, and it is true that the king as well as the main funerary divinities have at least one chapel there. However, on the walls there are also pictures of the great gods of the kingdom (among others, *Amun*) as well as of other divinities whose primary roles are by no means connected to the afterlife. It may be that this expresses a desire to associate the destiny of Pharaoh with that of the gods in order to emphasize his identification with the god *Amun-Re'*, the supreme manifestation of the sun.

The funerary temples and cults are the result of a specific and fairly complicated logic. In Egypt, contrary to what is often believed elsewhere, it is not the living who have anything to fear from the dead, but rather the dead who depend on the living. Death is, in fact, only a stage on

the road to a new existence, that of the body in its tomb, whereas the soul moves into the statue of the ka (sustaining spirit) of the deceased. It amounts to a kind of copy of life since, the second existence is a replica of the first one and consists in doing the same work: eating, drinking, sleeping, etc. However, what is most to be feared is a second death, which will be definitive. The deceased can escape this horrible fate only if he is regularly supplied with food and drink, without which no living creature can subsist: this is the role of the funerary cult.

"Castles of Millions of Years"

On the west bank of the Nile, across from the temples of **Karnak** and **Luxor**, stands the Theban "City of the Dead" containing everything that the New Kingdom could imagine in order to care for its deceased: royal and civil tombs, cut into the rock, and funerary temples, commonly called "Castles of Millions of Years," built on the edges of the desert or in rocky cirques. Most of the kings from the 18th, 19th and 20th dynasties built a sanctuary for themselves near the necropolis. Some of these sanctuaries no longer exist, lost through negligence or recycling of the building materials; others count among the masterpieces of Egyptian architecture.

Deir el-Bahri, the **"Convent of the North,"** gets its name from a monastery installed within its walls in the Christian era. It is built at the foot of the western cliff in a rocky cirque where the temple of queen ***Hatshepsut*** seems to grow out of the rock. No other construction is as perfectly integrated into its natural environment; it is, doubtlessly, the most remarkable monument in the whole necropolis, by the choice of the site, the perfection of its proportions, the originality of its plan and the quality of its reliefs engraved on very pure limestone.

It was designed by the architect **Senenmut** and rises up in terraces linked by a central ramp and lined with colonnades decorated with bas-reliefs. The temple was dedicated to the supreme god of the kingdom, *Amun*, but certain parts of it were reserved for *Hathor*, *Anubis* and Re'-*Harakhty*. It was also used for the funerary cults of the queen and her parents, ***Tuthmosis I*** and ***Ahmes***. The lower terrace ends in a colonnade with two rows of pillars, interrupted in the middle by the access ramp leading to the upper terrace. The decorations show scenes of royal hunting and fishing parties as well as of the ceremony at the setting-up of the queen's two obelisks in the temple of *Amun* at **Karnak**. The middle terrace has a similar layout: two colonnades on each side of the ramp leading to the upper level. Here, the reliefs tell the story of ***Hatshepsut***'s divine birth, her education, her co-regency with her father, ***Tuthmosis I***, and finally, her accession to the throne as the sole "king." Further along, there are scenes from the naval expedition to the **Land of Punt** (South of the Red Sea), organized in Year 9 of her reign to bring back various products unobtainable in Egypt: gold, precious stones, felines, incense, monkeys, giraffes, ebony, ivory, myrrh, skins, aromatic oils, etc. The funniest scene is the one of the queen of **Punt**, fat and misshapen, preceding her servants. Is it caricature or realism? Nobody knows. At the end of the north colonnade and cut out of the rock, lies the chapel of the mummification god, *Anubis*, consisting of an antechamber and three adjoining sanctuaries that still have their bright colors and remain in a perfect state of conservation.

Deir el-Bahri

No pharaonic construction is so well integrated into its natural environment as the "Castle of Millions of Years" of queen Hatshepsut. It seems as if the cliff had been modeled to provide a space for the temple. The creator of this splendid complex is Senenmut: he was the queen's chief architect, tutor to the royal princess Neferuret, and held a position of authority in the government. To serve the funerary cult of the queen, he designs a terraced temple where two successive ramps lead to the chapels dedicated to the gods of the kingdom and to Hatshepsut as a divinity. Apart from the wonderful architectural design, the reliefs carved on the colonnades count among the greatest masterpieces of Egyptian art. The depicted scenes are scarcely traditional: the journey to the Land of Punt, divine birth of Hatshepsut, ceremony at the setting-up of the obelisks in the temple at Karnak, etc.
[Temple of queen Hatshepsut, Deir el-Bahri, West Thebes, Upper Egypt].

The colossi of Memnon

These colossal statues of Amenhotep III that stand alone among the fields, are intriguing because of their isolation. In fact, they decorated the front of his funerary temple of which only a few scattered stones remain. It is probable that the stones of his temple were recovered and used in other constructions. The mutilation of the faces is probably due to the systematic destruction perpetrated in the Armanian period. The statues are 63 feet high. Each one is cut out of a single sandstone block brought from Heliopolis, 420 miles away. These statues became famous fairly late. The texts explain that in 27 B.C., a terrible earthquake cracked the northern colossus. From then on, the statue started to vibrate or "sing" just after daybreak when the temperature and humidity changed abruptly. People came from near and far to hear the strange whistling sound and find a logical explanation. Little by little, a legend grew up: the sound was the lamentations by Memnon, the Ethiopian king killed by Achilles in the Trojan war, as he greeted his mother Eos, the dawn. The "Colossus of Memnon" became the site of a pilgrimage and people came to listen to him at sunrise, arriving early so as not to miss the very short instant when the lament of the hero could be heard. In the third century A.D., the Roman emperor, Septimus Severus, wanted to restore the colossus and decided to repair the damaged torso and head by adding some sandstone blocks. The laments were never heard again but the colossus kept its name.

[Colossi of Memnon,
West Thebes, Upper Egypt.]

At the opposite end, the chapel of *Hathor* has two halls, whose columns are topped by cow-headed capitals, and a chapel with three small annexes. Queen ***Hatshepsut***'s chief architect, **Senenmut** has not hesitated to add a portrait of himself here and, even more unusual, to write his name. Regarding the upper terrace, which is very damaged and has been inaccessible for a long time, it included a courtyard, a colonnade, secondary chapels and a sanctuary, cut deeply into the cliff and dedicated to the queen.

If we believe **Diodorus of Sicily**, the Greek historian from the 1st century B.C., the **"tomb of Ozymandias"** was a marvelous monument. Unfortunately, it is now so damaged that one cannot form an opinion of it and it is difficult to imagine how vast this complex might have been, since all of the outer walls have disappeared and the main part of the remaining constructions have fallen down. Nowadays, the name **Ramesseum** is more commonly used to identify the funerary temple of ***Ramesses II***.

Two spacious courtyards preceded by pylons, lead to the great columned hall from which one has access to three other, smaller hypostyle halls and a sanctuary surrounded by annexes, crypts and chambers. A thick brick wall surrounds the complex and abuts another, still fairly complete collection of stables, storehouses and vaulted living quarters.

In the first courtyard, only the colossal, monolithic statue of ***Ramesses II*** deserves particular notice. Apart from the **"Colossi of Memnon"** there is no other statue, carved in Egypt, of this magnitude which demonstrates the megalomania of the king. It is 57 feet high, the face is 6 feet wide from ear to ear, the chest is 23 feet wide, the diameter of the arm is 5 feet, the index finger 3 feet long and it weighs 1,000 tons! There is nothing left of the second courtyard except a few colossi of the sovereign as *Osiris*, arms crossed on his chest and holding the **heka** scepter and the flail, **flagellum**, and some very beautiful fragments of two black granite statues. On the ground lies a head, a magnificent portrait of ***Ramesses II***.

The access to the, slightly raised, great pillared hall is by a ramp divided into three flights of steps. Of the original forty-eight columns, only twenty-nine remain to hold up part of the ceiling. On each side of the entrance door to what remains of the sanctuary, the lower part of the wall is decorated with a double procession of the sons and daughters of ***Ramesses II***, ranked according to age. His successor, king ***Merneptah***, is only in 18th place, which shows how many of his children died before him. Of the three following halls and the sanctuary, only the first one is interesting because of the original decorations on its ceiling: astronomical scenes representing the gods of the constellations, of the stars and of the zodiac.

The temple of Sethos I at Abydos

Situated between **Asyut** and **Thebes**, the site of **Abydos** includes various temples, necropolises and shrines from all periods. The religious importance of this city has very ancient roots. In the first dynasties, kings and high officials were buried here and at the end of the Old Kingdom, the cult of *Osiris* is introduced because, according to the texts, the head of the dismembered god is kept on this site. Thus, **Abydos** rapidly becomes the most important holy city in the country, where every self-respecting Egyptian must go on a pilgrimage once in his lifetime.

In the 19th dynasty, ***Sethos I*** decides to put two buildings inside the same wall: a sanctuary and a tomb, that of *Osiris*, also called **Osireion**. There is, in fact, no word that correctly expresses the function of this sanctuary. It is neither, properly speaking, a funerary temple (as his own is in the Theban necropols at **Gurna**) nor a cult temple. It is rather as if ***Sethos I*** had left, as a kind of ex voto, an admirable and very original structure, just as a private person would put up a stela in memory of his pilgrimage.

The temple was dedicated to seven gods who consequently needed as many chapels next to each other, which could either be used separately or at the same time. The plan devised to solve the problem of this multitude of parallel cults was quite original since it divided the entire temple, from the outer courtyards to the chapels, into seven parts.

Today, the second courtyard, closed by a great colonnade, has become the front of the temple, since the first pylon no longer exists. In the initial structure, this colonnade had seven gates that allowed the processions to proceed to the seven chapels, but ***Ramesses II*** decided to close all but the central gate. When one has passed

through this gate, the division of the temple into seven parts becomes very clear. Two hypostyle halls succeed each other; each one has seven doors leading to the seven chapels, dedicated to ***Sethos I*** divinized, *Ptah*, *Re'-Harakhty*, *Amun*, *Isis*, *Osiris* and *Horus*. After the ceremonies the barges of the gods were stored here. The hall reserved for *Osiris* gives access to two chapels honoring *Isis*, *Osiris* and *Horus*. On the opposite side, a long corridor from the second columned hall leads to chapels dedicated to *Ptah-Sokar-Osiris* and *Nefertem*.

All these rooms, decorated by **Sethos I**, are remarkable because of their beautiful reliefs, more graceful and pure than anything found elsewhere. Some of them still have their original paint and show how colorful the temples must have been in pharaonic times. A few, very classical, scenes depict the pharaoh making offerings to the gods, others, fewer in number, tell different stories from the **"Legend of Osiris."** The lasting impression is of the profound piety of the king as he bows down in front of the god in a gesture of veneration.

A FEW MILESTONES

THINITE PERIOD ***3150 to 2686 B.C.***

Egypt is united under the authority of a single king. Religion, government, art and script are fixed in nearly final form. Exploration of foreign countries begins.

OLD KINGDOM ***2686 TO 2181 B.C.***

This is the great period of classical Egypt. The kings choose **Memphis** as their capital and Egypt reaches an exceptional degree of refinement. Stone buildings make their appearance and soon the pharaohs start constructing pyramids in which to be buried: at **Saqqara** (***Djoser***) at **Dahshur** (***Sneferu***) and at **Giza** (***Khufu***, ***Khephren*** and ***Menkaure***).

In the 6th Dynasty, the royal authority declines as provincial governments gain power; the offices become hereditary and real dynasties are established, sometimes becoming more powerful than the Pharaoh himself. The governors become independent and Egypt seems threatened by foreign invaders. The royal authority, weakened by the too long reign of ***Pepy II***, lacks the power to redress the situation and the country sinks into a period of turmoil.

FIRST INTERMEDIATE PERIOD ***2181 TO 2060 B.C.***

Complete anarchy prevails: a multitude of petty kings seize power, the nobility is deprived of their property, the land lies fallow and famine rapidly follows.

MIDDLE KINGDOM ***2060 TO 1782 B.C.***

The Theban princes manage to reunite Egypt under a single authority. In Year 15 of his reign, ***Mentuhotpe*** becomes king of Upper and Lower Egypt. This new era of prosperity, presided over by the ***Senusret*** and the ***Amenemhet*** brings a number of political, administrative and religious reforms.

Economic progress is associated with the colonizing of new territories in **Sinai**, **Nubia** and **el-Faiyum**, the western and eastern deserts. Nevertheless, the 12th Dynasty ends in famine, turmoil, internecine disputes and foreign invasions whose reasons remain obscure.

SECOND INTERMEDIATE PERIOD ***1782 TO 1570 B.C.***

It seems quite clear that the arrival of the **Hyksos**, the "Chiefs of Foreign Countries", destabilized the country. They reigned sometimes over Lower Egypt and sometimes over the entire country from their capital **Avaris** in the north-east of the Delta, but at the beginning of the 17th dynasty the Theban princes adopt the royal titulary and go to war against the invaders.

NEW KINGDOM ***1570 TO 1070 B.C.***

This kingdom marks a new era of prosperity and refinement: renewal of royal authority, great territorial expansion, influx of wealth into Egypt. As their capital the kings adopt **Thebes**, "The City of a Hundred Gates" which becomes a symbol of prosperity, riches and luxury. This is the splendid era of ***Tuthmosis*** and ***Amenhotep***, Queen ***Hatshepsut***, the heretic couple ***Akhenaten*** and ***Nefertiti***, the young ***Tutankhamun***, Kings ***Sethos*** and ***Ramesses***.

However, the increasing importance of the clergy and religion in the affairs of state undermine the royal authority. The kingdom is weakened by loss of power and internecine strife and is no longer capable of fending off the invaders threatening its borders. This slow decay is to prove fatal to Egypt.

THIRD INTERMEDIATE PERIOD ***1070 TO 656 B.C.***

Egypt deteriorates slowly but inexorably. Outside threats combine with interior unrest. In the 21st and 22nd Dynasties, the Theban clergy reign in the South while Pharaoh settles in **Tanis** and rules over the North. The 25th dynasty is Ethiopian: ***Piy***, king of **Napata**, seizes power and gradually subjugates the South. His successor, ***Shabaqo***, chooses **Thebes** as his capital and, from there, he conquers the Delta.

LATE PERIOD ***656 TO 332 B.C.***

This period heralds the end of independence for pharaonic Egypt. Wars, conspiracies, invasions and foreign dynasties follow each other in rapid succession. Only the 30th Dynasty initiated by ***Nectanebo I*** manages to revive the past glory of Egypt. In 351 B.C. ***Nectanebo II*** wards off a Persian onslaught but, ten years later ***Artaxerxes III*** conquers the country a second time: he invades the country, routs ***Nectanebo II*** and establishes the 31st dynasty, called the "Second Persian Period."

PTOLEMAIC PERIOD ***332 TO 30 B.C.***

In 333 B.C. ***Alexander the Great*** arrives in Egypt and defeats the Persian invaders. He founds the city of **Alexandria** and entrusts the government of the country to a prefect. At his death, Egypt passes to one of his lieutenants, ***Ptolemy***, who eventually adopts the royal titulary and initiates the Ptolemaic dynasty. Fourteen ***Ptolemies*** succeed each other on the Egyptian throne, and the dynasty ends with the reign of Queen ***Cleopatra***.

In 31 B.C., the battle of **Actium** is lost by ***Marcus Antonius*** and followed by the invasion of the legions of ***Octavius***. After ***Antonius***' suicide, ***Cleopatra*** delivers **Alexandria** into the hands of the conqueror and, after having tried in vain to seduce him, kills herself. Egypt becomes a Roman province.

CHRONOLOGY

Early Dynastic Period 3150-2686 B.C.

1st Dynasty
Narmer
Aha
Djer
Djet
Den
Semerkhet
Qa'a

2nd Dynasty
Hetepsekhemwy
Raneb
Nynetjer
Peribsen
Khasekhemwy

Old Kingdom 2686-2181 B.C.

3rd Dynasty
Sanakht
Djoser
Sekhemket
Khaba
Huni

4th Dynasty
Sneferu
Khufu
Djedefra
Khephren
Menkaure
Shepseskaf

5th Dynasty
Userkaf
Sahura
Neferirkara-Kakai
Shepsaskara
Raneferef
Nyuserra
Menkauhor
Djedkara
Unas

6th Dynasty
Teti
Pepy I
Merenra
Pepy II

First Intermediate Period 2181 - 2060 B.C.

7th Dynasty *(totally unknown)*

8th Dynasty *(from Memphis)*
Wadjkara
Kakara Ibi

9th and 10th Dynasties *(from Herakleopolis)*
Khety I
Merykara
Neferkara
Khety II

11th Dynasty *(Theban and contemporary with the end of the 10th Dynasty)*
Mentuhotpe I
Intef I
Intef II
Intef III

Middle Kingdom 2 060 - 1 782 B.C.

11th Dynasty
Mentuhotpe II
Mentuhotpe III
Mentuhotpe IV

12th Dynasty
Amenemhet I
Senusret I
Amenemhet II
Senwuret II
Senwuret III
Amenemhet III
Amenemhet IV
Sobekneferu

Second Intermediate Period 1782 - 1570 B.C.

13th Dynasty *(a dynasty during which the kings, who are native Egyptians, seem still to reign over the two kingdoms of Egypt, the capital of which is in Iti-Tawi, in the oasis of el-Faiyum)*
Wegaf
Intef IV
Hor
Sebekhotpe II
Khendjer
Sebekhotpe III
Neferhotpe I
Sebekhotpe IV
Aya
Neferhotpe II

14th Dynasty *(contemporary with the end of the 13th Dynasty, which ends in an obscure fashion; the 14th Dynasty only reigns over the eastern part of the Delta)*
Nehesy

15th and 16th Dynasties *(Hyksos dynasties: these kings, coming from the East, take power in Egypt and set up their capital in Avaris)*
Sharek
Yakub-Har
Khyan
Apepi I
Apepi II
Anather
Yakobaam

17th Dynasty *(Theban Dynasty, who tried to win back the land by driving out the Hyksos)*
Sebekemsaf II
Intef VII
Taa I
Taa II
Kamose

New Kingdom
1570 - 1070 B. C.

18th Dynasty	Ahmose
	Amenhotep I
	Tuthmosis I
	Tuthmosis II
	Hatshepsut
	Tuthmosis III
	Amenhotep II
	Tuthmosis IV
	Amenhotep III
	Amenhotep IV-Akhenaten
	Smenkhkara
	Tutankhamun
	Ay
	Horemheb
19th Dynasty	Ramesses I
	Sethos I
	Ramesses II
	Merneptah
	Amenmessu
	Sethos II
	Siptah
	Tausret
20th Dynasty	Sethnakhte
	Ramesses III
	Ramesses IV-Ramesses XI

Third Intermediate Period
1070 - 656 B. C.

21st Dynasty *(two contemporary kingdoms: the priests kings usurp the cartouche and reign in Thebes over Upper Egypt, whereas in the Delta, Smendes proclaims himself king at the death of Ramesses XI, sets up his capital in Tanis and reigns over Lower Egypt)*

Tanis	**Thebes**
Smendes I	Herihor
Amenemnisu	Piankh
Psusennes I	Pinedjem I
Amenemope	Masaharta
Osorkon the Elder	Menkheperre'
Siamun	Smendes II
Psusennes II	Pinedjem II

22nd Dynasty *(Lybian dynasty, coming from Bubastis and reigning in Tanis)*

Sheshonq I
Osorkon I
Sheshonq II
Takelot I
Osorkon II
Takelot II
Sheshonq III
Pimay
Sheshonq V
Osorkon IV
Harsiesis

23rd Dynasty *(contemporary with the end of the 22nd Dynasty, the first ruling in the Delta over Lower Egypt, and the second ruling in Leontopolis over Middle Egypt)*

Pedubastis I
Sheshonq IV
Osorkon III
Takelot III
Rudamon
Iuput

24th Dynasty *(first Dynasty of Sais)*

Tefnakht
Bocchoris

25th Dynasty *(from Nubia: the kings of Napata take over the rule in Egypt)*

Piy
Shabaqo
Shabitqo
Taharqo
Tanutamani

Late Period
664 - 332 B.C.

26th Dynasty *(second Dynasty of Sais)*

Psamtek I
Nekau
Psamtek II
Apries
Ahmose
Psamtek III

27th Dynasty *(first Persian rule)*

Cambyses
Darius I
Xerxes
Artaxerxes I
Darius II
Artaxerxes II

28th Dynasty	Amyrtaios
29th Dynasty	Nepherites I
	Hakor
30th Dynasty	Nectanebo I
	Teos
	Nectanebo II

31st Dynasty *(second Persian rule)*

Artaxerxes III
Arses
Darius III Codoman

332-323 B.C. *In 332 B.C., Alexander the Great enters into Egypt and frees the country of the Persian rule by chasing Darius III away. At his death in 323, Egypt passes under the government of one of his lieutenants, Ptolemy, who takes the title of pharaoh in 305 and founds the Ptolemaic dynasty.*

305-30 B.C.	**Ptolemaic Dynasty**
	Ptolemy I Soter I
	Ptolemy II Philadelphus
	Ptolemy III Euergetes I
	Ptolemy IV Philopator
	Ptolemy V Epiphanes
	Ptolemy VI Philometor
	Ptolemy VII Neos Philopator
	Ptolemy VIII Euergetes II
	Ptolemy IX Soter II
	Ptolemy X Alexander I
	Ptolemy XI Alexander II
	Ptolemy XII Neos Dionysos
	Ptolemy XIII and Cleopatra VII
	Ptolemy XIV and Cleopatra VII
	Cleopatra VII

30 B.C. - 395 A.D. - Roman Egypt

HIEROGLYPHS

Three classes of signs need to be distinguished in the hieroglyphic writing: the **phonograms**, the **logograms** and the **determinatives**.

9/10ths of the system are **phonograms** which have a sound value and can be divided into three groups: *uniconsonantal* signs (one sign has the value of a consonant or semi-consonant), *biconsonantal* signs (one sign has the value of two consonants or semi-consonants) or *triconsonantal* signs (one sign has the value of three consonants or semi-consonants). The *biconsonantal* and *triconsonantal* signs are accompanied by one or several *uniconsonantal* signs, the *phonetic complements*, used to reinforce the phonetic value of the signs they go with.

The **logograms** represent a concept and allow to note it through an individual sign whose meaning is broadly equivalent to his appearance (a boat for "boat").

The **determinatives** are not pronounced but qualify the word which precedes them; they are put behind the word they determine.

Before deciphering a text in hieroglyphs, the translator must give a phonetic value to the signs. This preliminary task of ***transliteration*** is absolutely necessary to be able to pronounce the Egyptian words. But the hieroglyphic writing, just as its transliteration, only uses consonants or semi-consonants what makes the proper pronounciation impossible to establish. So, to be able to pronounce the words, one must add vowels between the consonants or transform semi-consonants into vowels.

Egyptian language can be written from high to low, right to left or left to right (what we use for convenience), never from low to high. The sense of lecture is indicated by the signs representing animals or people; if they look at the left, we read from left to right, and vice versa. In the inscriptions, signs are situated in an harmonious more than in a logical way. The scribe works gathering and situating the signs, which can be vertical, horizontal or square, according to their shape.

Uniconsonantal signs

Vulture
Pronunciation: **a**
Transliteration: *3*

Reed in flower
Pronunciation: **i**
Transliteration: *i*

Double reed in flower
Pronunciation: **y**
Transliteration: *y*

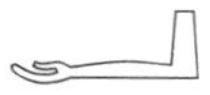

Forearm
Pronunciation: **a**
Transliteration: *ᶜ*

Quail chick
Pronunciation: **ou**
Transliteration: *w*

Leg
Pronunciation: **b**
Transliteration: *b*

Seat
Pronunciation: **p**
Transliteration: *p*

Horned viper
Pronunciation: **f**
Transliteration: *f*

Owl
Pronunciation: **m**
Transliteration: *m*

Dash of water or **crown**
Pronunciation: **n**
Transliteration: *n*

Mouth
Pronunciation: **r**
Transliteration: *r*

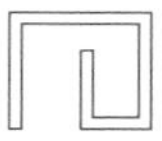

Building plan
Pronunciation: **h**
Transliteration: *h*

Wick of linen
Pronunciation: **h** emphatic
Transliteration: *ḥ*

Placenta (?)
Pronunciation: **kh** (jota)
Transliteration: *ḫ*

Cow vulva (?)
Pronunciation: **ç**
Transliteration: *h*

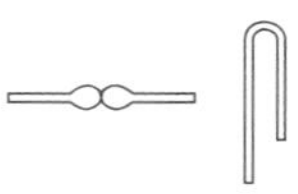

Bolt or **linen**
Pronunciation: **s** (muffled)
Transliteration: *s*

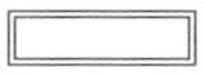

Pool
Pronunciation: **ch**
Transliteration: *š*

Hill slope
Pronunciation: **k**
Transliteration: *ḳ*

Basket with handle
Pronunciation: **k**
Transliteration: *k*

Jar prop
Pronunciation: **g** (hard)
Transliteration: *g*

Loaf of bread
Pronunciation: **t**
Transliteration: *t*

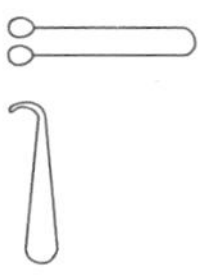

Rope or pestle
Pronunciation: **tch**
Transliteration: *ṯ*

Hand
Pronunciation: **d**
Transliteration: *d*

Cobra
Pronunciation: **dj**
Transliteration: *ḏ*

A few biconsonantal signs

Coiled lasso Pronunciation: **wa** Transliteration: ***wa***	**Vase** Pronunciation: **nu** Transliteration: ***nw***	**Human eye** Pronunciation: **ir** Transliteration: ***ir***
Bird in flight Pronunciation: **pa** Transliteration: ***p3***	**Recumbent lion** Pronunciation: **ru** Transliteration: ***rw***	**Plan of a house** Pronunciation: **per** Transliteration: ***pr***
Scythe Pronunciation: **ma** Transliteration: ***m3***	**Ostrich feather** Pronunciation: **chu** Transliteration: ***šw***	**Hoe** Pronunciation: **mer** Transliteration: ***mr***
Duck Pronunciation: **sa** Transliteration: ***s3***	**Double mountain** Pronunciation: **dju** Transliteration: ***ḏw***	**Face seen from the front** Pronunciation: **her** Transliteration: ***ḥr***
Lifted arms Pronunciation: **ka** Transliteration: ***k3***	**Sledge** Pronunciation: **toum** Transliteration: ***tm***	**Knotted fox skins** Pronunciation: **mes** Transliteration: ***ms***
Tool for fire Pronunciation: **dja** Transliteration: ***ḏ3***	**Rabbit** Pronunciation: **oun** Transliteration: ***wn***	**Throne** Pronunciation: **set** Transliteration: ***st***
Three dashes of water Pronunciation: **mu** Transliteration: ***mw***	**Checkerboard** Pronunciation: **men** Transliteration: ***mn***	**Everlasting Pillar** Pronunciation: **djed** Transliteration: ***ḏd***
Animal's thorax Pronunciation: **au** Transliteration: ***3w***	**Basket** Pronunciation: **neb** Transliteration: ***nb***	**Vulture** Pronunciation: **met/mut** Transliteration: ***mt/mwt***

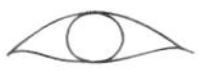

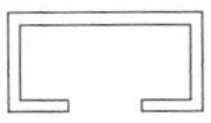

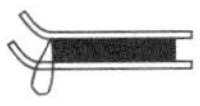

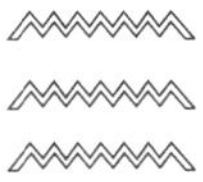

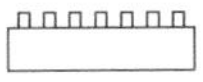

A few triconsonantal signs

Sign of life Pronunciation: **ankh** Transliteration: ***ᶜnḫ***	**Heart and trachea** Pronunciation: **nefer** Transliteration: ***nfr***	**Scarab** Pronunciation: **khéper** Transliteration: ***ḫpr***
Mast Pronunciation: **aha** Transliteration: ***ᶜḥᶜ***	**Stick wrapped in cloth** Pronunciation: **netcher** Transliteration: ***nṯr***	**Three libation vases** Pronunciation: **khenet** Transliteration: ***ḫnt***
Column, pillar Pronunciation: **ioun** Transliteration: ***iwn***	**Carob shell** Pronunciation: **nedjem** Transliteration: ***nḏm***	**Lungs** Pronunciation: **sema** Transliteration: ***sm3***
Broom Pronunciation: **wah** Transliteration: ***w3ḥ***	**Palm branch** Pronunciation: **renep** Transliteration: ***rnp***	**Axe on a block** Pronunciation: **setep** Transliteration: ***stp***
Jackal-headed scepter Pronunciation: **usir** Transliteration: ***wsr***	**Bread on a mat** Pronunciation: **hetep** Transliteration: ***ḥtp***	**Trap** Pronunciation: **guereg** Transliteration: ***grg***

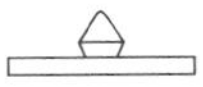

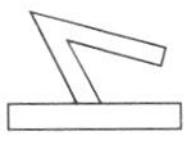

KINGS OF EGYPT

Ahmose
The moon is born

Nebpehtyre
The Lord of Strength is Re'

Tomb : without certainty, vault at **Dra Abu el-Naga** (West Thebes, Upper Egypt)

Akhenaten
Servant of the Aten

Neferkheperure
Beautiful are the Manifestations of Re'

Tomb : without certainty, hypogeum at **Akhetaton** (Middle Egypt)

Amenemhet I
Amun is at the Head

Sehetepibre
Satisfied is the Heart of Re'

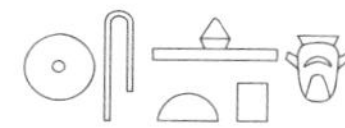

Tomb : pyramid at **el-Lisht** (Road of the pyramids, Lower Egypt)

Amenemhet II
Amun is at the Head

Nubkaure
Golden are the souls of Re'

Tomb : pyramid at **Dahshur** (Road of the pyramids, Lower Egypt)

Amenemhet III
Amun is at the Head

Nymaatre
Belonging to the Justice of Re'

Tomb : pyramids at **Dahshur** and at **Hawara** (Road of the pyramids, Lower Egypt)

Amenhotep I
Amun is Pleased

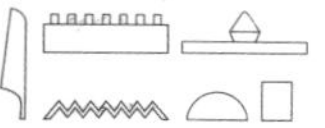

Djeserkare
Holy is the soul of Re'

Tomb : hypogeum n°39 (**?**) of the **Valley of the Kings** (West Thebes, Upper Egypt)

Amenhotep II
Amun is Pleased

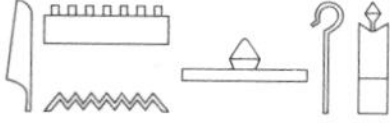

Akheperure
Great are the Manifestations of Re'

Tomb : hypogeum n°35 of the **Valley of the Kings** (West Thebes, Upper Egypt)

Amenhotep III
Amun is Pleased

Nebmaatre
Lord of the Truth is Re'

Tomb : hypogeum n°22 of the **Valley of the Kings** (West Thebes, Upper Egypt)

Ay
Ay, Father of the God

Kheperkheperure
Everlasting are the Manifestations of Re'

Tomb : hypogeum n°23 of the **Valley of the Kings** (West Thebes, Upper Egypt)

Hatshepsut
Foremost of Noble Ladies

Maatkare
Truth is the Soul of Re'

Tomb : hypogeum n°20 of the **Valley of the Kings** (West Thebes, Upper Egypt)

Horemheb
Horus is in Jubilation, Beloved of Amun

Djeserkheperure Setepenre
Holy are the Manifestations of Re', Chosen of Re'

Tomb : hypogeum n°57 of the **Valley of the Kings** (West Thebes, Upper Egypt)

Khephren
Appearing like Re'

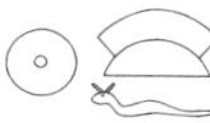

Tomb : pyramid at **Giza** (Road of the pyramids, Lower Egypt)

Khufu
Protected by Khnum

Tomb : pyramid at **Giza** (Road of the pyramids, Lower Egypt)

Menkaure
Eternal like the Souls of Re'

Tomb : pyramid at **Giza** (Road of the pyramids, Lower Egypt)

Merneptah
Beloved of Ptah, Joyous is Truth

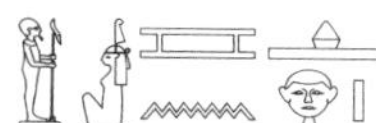

Baenre Merynetjeru
The Soul of Re', Beloved of the gods

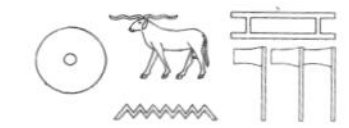

Tomb : hypogeum n°8 of the **Valley of the Kings** (West Thebes, Upper Egypt)

Montuhotpe II
Montu is Content

Nebhepetre
Pleased is the Lord of Re'

Tomb : tomb at **Deir el-Bahri** (West Thebes, Upper Egypt)

Osorkon the Elder
Osorkon

Aakheperre Setepenre
Great is the soul of Re', Chosen of Re'

Tomb : unknowm

Pepy I
Pepy

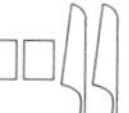

Meryre
Beloved of Re'

Tomb : pyramid at **South Saqqara** (Road of the pyramids, Lower Egypt)

Pepy II **Neferkare**
Pepy *Beautiful is the Soul of Re'*

Tomb : pyramid at **South Saqqara** (Road of the pyramids, Lower Egypt)

Psusennes I **Akheperre Setepenimen**
The Star that appears in the City *Great are the Actions of Re', Chosen of Amun*

Tomb : royal necropolis of **Tanis** (Delta of the Nile, Lower Egypt)

Ramesses I **Menpehtyre**
Re' has Fashioned Him *Eternal is the Strengh of Re'*

Tomb : hypogeum n°16 of the **Valley of the Kings** (West Thebes, Upper Egypt)

Ramesses II **Usermaatre Setepenre**
Re' has Fashioned Him, Beloved of Amun *The Justice of Re' is Powerful, Chosen of Re'*

Tomb : hypogeum n°7 of the **Valley of the Kings** (West Thebes, Upper Egypt)

Ramesses III **Ousermaâtrê Méryimen**
Re' has Fashioned Him, Ruler of Heliopolis - Powerful is the Justice of Re', Beloved of Amun

Tomb : hypogeum n°11 of the **Valley of the Kings** (West Thebes, Upper Egypt)

Senusret I **Kheperkare**
Man of the goddess Wosret *The Soul of Re' comes into Being*

Tomb : pyramid at **el-Lisht** (Road of the pyramids, Lower Egypt)

Senusret II **Khakheperre**
Man of the goddess Wosret *The Transformation of Re' appears*

Tomb : pyramid at **el-Lahun** (Road of the pyramids, Lower Egypt)

Senusret III **Khakaure**
Man of the goddess Wosret *Appearing like the Souls of Re'*

Tomb : pyramid at **Dashur** (Road of the pyramids, Lower Egypt)

Sethos I Merneptah **Menmaatre**
He of the god Seth, Beloved of Ptah *Eternal is the Justice of Re'*

Tomb : hypogeum n°17 of the **Valley of the Kings** (West Thebes, Upper Egypt)

Sethos II Merneptah **Userkheperure Setepenre**
He of the god Seth, Beloved of Ptah - Powerful are the Manifestations of Re', Chosen by Re'

Tomb : hypogeum n°15 of the **Valley of the Kings** (West Thebes, Upper Egypt)

Sheshonq I **Hedjkheperre Setepenre**
Sheshonq, Beloved of Amun *Bright is the Manifestations of Re', Chosen of Re'*

Tomb : without certainty, royal necropolis of **Tanis** (Delta of the Nile, Lower Egypt)

Smenkhkara **Ankhkheperure**
Vigorous is the Soul of Re' *Leaving are the Manifestations of Re'*

Tomb : hypogeum n°55 (?) of the **Valley of the Kings** (West Thebes, Upper Egypt)

Sneferu
He of Beauty

Tomb : two pyramids at **Dashur** (Road of the pyramids, Lower Egypt)

Tutankhamun **Nebkheperure**
Living image of Amun *Lord of the Manifestations is Re'*

Tomb : hypogeum n°62 of the **Valley of the Kings** (West Thebes, Upper Egypt)

Tuthmosis I **Akheperkare**
Born of the god Thoth *Great is the Soul of Re'*

Tomb : hypogeum n°20 / 38 of the **Valley of the Kings** (West Thebes, Upper Egypt)

Tuthmosis II **Akheperenre**
Born of the god Thoth *Great is the Form of Re'*

Tomb : hypogeum n°42 (?) of the **Valley of the Kings** (West Thebes, Upper Egypt)

Tuthmosis III **Menkheperre**
Born of the god Thoth *Lasting is the Manifestations of Re'*

Tomb : hypogeum n°34 of the **Valley of the Kings** (West Thebes, Upper Egypt)

Tuthmosis IV **Menkheperure**
Born of the god Thoth *Everlasting are the Manifestations of Re'*

Tomb : hypogeum n°43 of the **Valley of the Kings** (West Thebes, Upper Egypt)

Unas
Unas

Tomb : pyramid at **North Saqqara** (Road of the pyramids, Lower Egypt)

Userkaf
His Soul is Powerful

Tomb : pyramid at **North Saqqara** (Road of the pyramids, Lower Egypt)

THE DIVINITIES

Amun

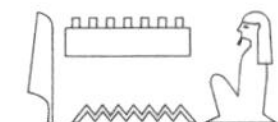

He originally comes from **Thebes**, but becomes the national and dynastic god from the Middle Kingdom on. His main place of worship is in **Thebes** (**Luxor** and **Karnak**) where he is venerated with the goddess *Mut* and the god son *Khons*.

Anubis

This funerary god, depicted as a black jackal or as a man with the head of a jackal, is supposed to be the inventor of mummification and makes sure the embalming ceremonies are properly conducted. He is, in a wider sense, the protector of the necropolis.

Anukis

She is the infant goddess of the **Elephantine** triad. With the god *Khnum* and the goddess *Satis*, she is guardian of the sources of the Nile and patroness of the cataract. She is depicted as a woman wearing a crown of feathers.

Apis

The sacred bull from **Memphis** is considered to be the representative of *Ptah* on earth. He is sometimes associated with *Osiris* and *Re'*; in this case, he adopts funerary and solar characteristics. The sacred bulls are buried in a particular necropolis called **Serapeums**.

Aten

He is the solar disc above all. He appears as early as the Old Kingdom period, but it is only under the 18th Dynasty that pharaoh ***Amenhotep IV-Akhenaten*** lifts him up as the only dynastic god.

Atum

He is one of the three forms of the creative and solar god of **Heliopolis**. *Atum* represents the setting sun, whereas *Re'* and *Khepri* are the moon and rising sun.

Bastet

This cat goddess, worshipped in the Delta at **Bubastis**, is the incarnation of the peaceful aspects of the dangerous goddesses. Her name is a symbol of joy and goodness, which is why her cult is so popular.

Bes

He is a domestic spirit, very popular in every household, considered to be the protector of children and women. His grotesque dances and horrible grimaces are supposed to drive out the evil spirits and hostile forces that haunt the houses.

Geb

He represents the earth and all the riches that are in the soil. With *Nut*, *Geb* forms the second divine couple of the great Heliopolitan Ennead.

Ha'py

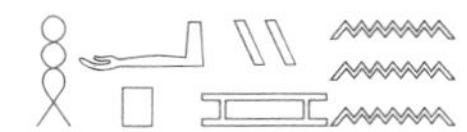

He represents the inundation and the flood of the Nile, which guarantee the fertility of cultivated fields. As a symbol of plenty, *Ha'py* is depicted as an androgynous deity, sometimes female and sometimes male, with hanging breasts.

Harakhty

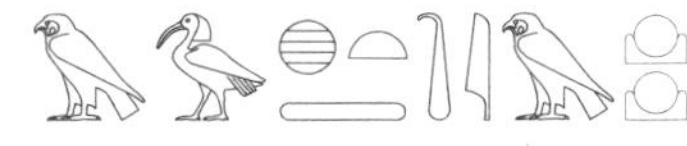

*"**Horus** of the Horizon"* is one of the forms of the creative and solar god from **Heliopolis**.

Hathor

She has all kinds of duties: she is goddess of beauty, love and joy, patroness of the Theban necropolis, celestial deity, mistress of the foreign lands, nurse of the royal child… She became so popular during the years that she acquires the personalities of other feminine deities, such as *Isis*.

Heqet

This goddess with a frog's head, is associated, in **Antinoe**, with the creative potter god, *Khnum*. When there is a union between a god and a royal wife, that is to say a theogamy, to give birth to a future king, she helps her divine husband shape the body of the infant.

Horus

He is the son of *Isis* and *Osiris*, who inherits from his grandfather, the god *Geb*, the kingdom of earth. *Horus* is the main dynastic god, and the pharaohs are under his direct protection. He is also a solar and a celestial god; as such, he is associated with the goddess *Hathor*.

Isis

She is wife and sister of *Osiris*, mother of *Horus*, and she has a very strong personality that confers many roles on her: protector of women and children, great magician, protector of the mummy of the deceased, universal goddess…

Khepri

He is the god honored in **Heliopolis** under the form of a dung beetle. He symbolizes the rising sun which is reborn every morning; with *Atum*, the setting sun, and *Re'*, the sun at noon, he is considered to be the creative god.

Khnum

This god with a ram's head has several places of worship. He is worshipped in **Elephantine** as the god of the cataract and the guardian of the sources of the Nile, in triad with *Satis* and *Anukis*. In **Esna**, he is the creative god; it is told that, on his potter's wheel, he has fashioned gods, men and objects

Khons

He is "the Wanderer" or "the Traveler," and is in direct relation with the moon. In the 18th Dynasty, he is associated with the god *Amun* and the goddess *Mut* as the god son of the Theban triad.

Ma'at

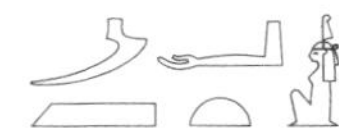

She symbolizes truth and justice. On earth, she guarantees cosmic balance and the universal order. In the afterworld, she determines the weight of the sins of the deceased. Men and gods have to obey her rule and respect what she incarnates.

Min

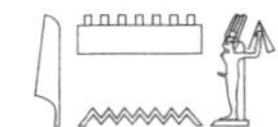

He is the god of fertility associated, in this role, with *Amun*, the god of the Kingdom. He is worshipped in **Coptos** and ***Akhmim*** as protector of the caravans and patron of the oriental desert tracks.

Montu

He is a falcon god from **Thebes**, who incarnates the irresistible force of war.

Mut 

In **Thebes**, this vulture goddess is the divine consort of *Amun* and the mother of the god *Khons*. She sometimes adopted the features of the warrior lion goddesses as *Sakhmet*.

Nefertem 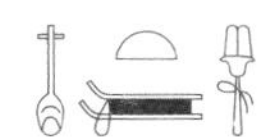

The sun emerged from this primeval lotus at the beginning of time. Several deities are associated with him: in **Memphis**, he is the son of *Ptah* and *Sakhmet*; in **Bubastis** the son of *Bastet*; in **Buto** the son of *Wadjit*.

Neith 

She has several functions: she is the warrior goddess of the town of **Sais** and demiurge of the town of **Esna**. In the underground world, she protects the **canopic jars** of the deceased with *Isis, Nephthys* and *Serket*.

Nekhbet 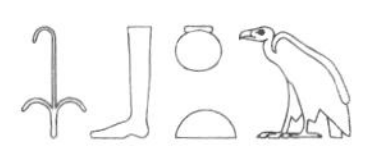

She is the vulture goddess of **El-Kab** and protector of Upper Egypt.

Nephthys 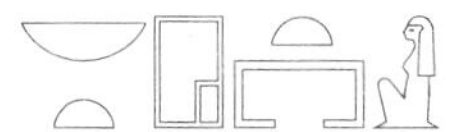

She belongs to the second generation of the gods of the Heliopolitan Ennead, with *Osiris*, *Isis, Horus the Elder* and *Seth*. Her role is essentially funerary, as she watches over the body of the deceased and his **canopic jars**.

Nun 

He is the primeval ocean that precedes creation in the cosmogonies: *"before the existence of the sky, before the existence of the earth, before the existence of men, before the existence of death"* was the *Nun*.

Nut 

She is the representation of the celestial vault. In the Heliopolitan cosmogony, she forms with *Geb*, the earth, the second divine couple. The day and night journey of the sun are made on her body, which is the symbol of the space through which the sun travels.

Osiris 

He is the god of the dead in the Egyptian pantheon, who also represents, because of his resurrection, the yearly revival of the vegetation. Everyone tries to identify himself with *Osiris* in the afterworld, and to enter his kingdom, since it is only he who can give hope of eternal life.

Ptah 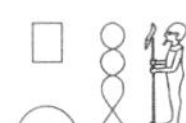

At the beginning, he is the patron of goldsmiths, sculptors and craftsmen; he is considered as the inventor of the technics. Afterwards, he becomes the creative god of **Memphis** in which triad he is the husband of *Sakhmet* and the father of *Nefertem*. In time he merges with *Sokar* and *Osiris* to form *Ptah-Sokar-Osiris*, and with *Tanen* to form *Ptah-Tanen*.

Re'  or 

He is pre-eminently the solar god, the most important deity of the Egyptian pantheon. His main place of worship is in **Heliopolis**, but he is worshipped throughout Egypt under many names: *Re'-Harakhty*, *Amun-Re'*, *Re'-Atum*, *Sobek-Re'*...

Sakhmet 

She is a power of destruction, incarnating the solar eye and dangerous forces. She is depicted as a goddess with the head of a lioness. She belongs to the Memphite triad, wife of *Ptah* and mother of *Nefertem*. In **Thebes**, she is assimilated to the goddess *Mut* as a healing goddess.

Satis 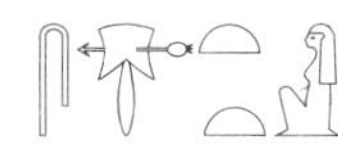

She is both guardian of the sources of the Nile and patroness of the cataract, associated with *Khnum* and *Anukis*.

Serket 

On earth, this scorpion goddess heals all kinds of bites and stings. In the afterworld, she is a protector of the viscera of the deceased, which are preserved in the **canopic jars**, with *Isis*, *Nephthys* and *Neith*.

Seshat 

She appears as the partner of *Thoth*, and in his company is mistress of mathematics and science, and patron of writing. She is said to keep the annals of the organized world, upon which are registered the royal feats of glory and main events of royalty.

Seth 

This god with the head of a mythical animal has many facets, some positive and some negative. He is at the same time the protector of the sun boat, and the murderer of *Osiris*. In the Late Period, he symbolizes "the Foreigner" and "the Destroyer": he is the force of Evil, the disorder and the trouble.

Shu 

With the goddess *Tefenet*, he forms the first divine couple of the Heliopolitan cosmogony. They both are born of the solar god, *Re'*, and allow him to reveal himself, thanks to their powers. *Shu* is particularly the god of space and air who symbolizes the breath of life.

Sobek 

The crocodile god has several places of worship, the most famous ones being in the region of **el-Faiyum** and in **Kom-Ombo**. In certain cases he is the creative god, but he is most often a protector of men against the wild beasts and hostile forces that live in the marshes and the waters of the Nile.

Tanen 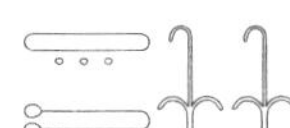

He is a very ancient Egyptian god. At the beginning, he is demiurge in **Memphis** and incarnates the first mound of earth that emerged from *Nun* at the beginning of the world. He is soon merged with *Ptah* to form *Ptah-Tanen*.

Taweret 

She has no particular place of worship, but is venerated in all Egyptian households as goddess protector of pregnant women and children.

Tefenet 

In the Heliopolitan tradition, she is the daughter of *Re'* and forms, with *Shu*, the vital breath, the first divine couple. She personifies the cosmic order and heat, without which the sun cannot reveal itself. She sometimes becomes "the Fearful One" and acquires the personality of the dangerous lion goddesses.

Thoth 

He is sometimes depicted as an ibis and sometimes as a baboon. He has many functions and many powers: he is the moon god, the inventor of writing and science, the protector of scribes, the master of knowledge, the divine messenger and book-keeper. In the afterworld, he is responsible for the proper weighing of hearts, and he writes down the verdict on the sacred scriptures.

Wadjit 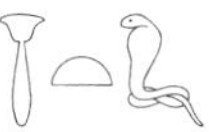

She is the cobra goddess of **Buto**, and protector of Lower Egypt.

LEXICON

Amulets - These objects are little figurines supposed to protect the living and the dead. Living Egyptians wear amulets as pendants, and the deceased have them placed in their linen wrappings. They are made of faience, precious or semi-precious stone, bronze, gold, silver… They either represent divinities or hieroglyphic signs full of meaning: the **djed** pillar (longevity and stability), the **ankh** cross (life), the **wedjat** eye (plenty), the **kheper** dung beetle (existence) or the **girdle of Isis** (protection in all circumstances).

Ba - Represented as a human-headed bird, the **ba**, the soul of the deceased in a way, is a kind of spirit that leaves the body at death and goes wandering as he likes: the **ba** can stay in the tomb near the body, go into the funerary chapel to appreciate the offerings or, even, can wander around to find the favorite walks of the deceased.

Beards - Although all respectable Egyptians are clean-shaven, gods, pharaohs and civil servants like to be represented wearing a false beard as a sign of their virility: the dieties are given long, slender, carefully braided ones turned up at the end, the kings have conical ones and the nobles a simple goatee.

Book of the Dead - Appearing from the New Kingdom on, this collection of texts, more correctly called the "**Book for Going Out by Day**", is a loose gathering of recipes that are supposed to secure the revival of the deceased in the afterworld, giving him complete freedom in his moves and giving everything he needs in the Underworld. The chapters, very often decorated with illustrations and vignettes, are written on a papyrus roll put into the coffin or inserted in the linen wrappings of the mummy. Many copies of this funerary book have been found, but they are all different, some have chapters that do not exist in others. To this day, there have been 190 different chapters recorded; they are numbered from I to CXC.

Canopic jars - The mummified viscera of the deceased are preserved in four canopic jars, made out of alabaster or limestone, and put under the protection of four gods, called the **four sons of Horus**, and four goddesses. *Hapy*, with a baboon's head, and *Nephthys* watch over the lungs; *Imset*, with a man's head, and *Isis* watch over the liver; *Qebehsenuf*, with a falcon's head, and *Serket* watch over the intestines; *Duamutef*, with a jackal's head, and *Neith* watch over the stomach.

Capitals - In Egypt several types of capitals were comonly used to crown the columns: palm-shaped, open or closed lotus flowers, papyrus heads, papyrus heads combined with other plants, Hathoric, i.e., human faces with cow's ears, representing the goddess *Hathor*.

Cartouche - This word designates the stretched out buckle symbolizing the universal reign of the king, and encircling the fourth and fifth names of the pharaohs: the **Throne name** (or **He of the Sedge and the Bee**) and the **Birth name** (or **Son of Re'**).

Coffin Texts - Contrary to the "**Pyramid texts**" only reserved to the royal person, these funerary texts are used by civilians and decorate the coffins during the Middle Kingdom. Issued from the democratisation of the funerary creeds, they allow the deceased to identify himself to *Osiris* in the afterworld, through spells and recipes aimed to deify the dead.

Consort - This word is used to qualify a goddess who is considered to be the wife of a god in a sanctuary. In the **Theban** triad, the goddess *Mut* is the consort of *Amun*, in the **Memphite** triad, *Sakhmet* is the consort of *Ptah*, in the **Elephantine** triad, *Satis* is the consort of *Khnum* and in the triad of **Abydos**, *Isis* is the consort of *Osiris*.

Dromos - The Greek gave this name to the alley that extends towards the outside the axis of a temple to link it to another one or to a landing on the Nile river. These alleys are often bordered with sphinxes or recumbent lions.

House of Life - This type of building, totally dependent on the temple activities, harbors various artisans who work for the sanctuary: scribes who compose or copy the sacred texts needed for artisans who work for the sanctuary: scribes who compose or copy the sacred texts needed for the cult; medical researchers or practitioners; celebrants and priests, craftsmen, decorators or teachers.

Hypogeum - This word designate a tomb, either royal or civilian, dug into a cliff.

Hypostyle - Any hall whose ceiling is supported by columns.

Ka - This notion is difficult to understand for there is no concept in our language for the Egyptian **ka**. It is considered to be a manifestation of vital energy, either conservative or creative, that continues to live after the death of the body. Offerings and funerary formulas are addressed to the **ka**, which is the element allowing the deceased to survive in the afterworld.

Laying foundations - When the foundations of religious or funerary constructions were laid, special rituals were performed: astronomic observations to determine the precise orientation, sacrifice of an animal whose carcass was placed in the foundation trench, deposition of miniature objects at the corners of the building (vases, tools, tablets, etc.).

Mammisi - The word is of coptic origin and its literal translation is "place of birth." It is the name of the buildings added to temples during the Late Period, where every year, the Egyptians celebrated the rites of the birth of the child-gods (*Nefertem*, *Khons*, etc.) and, by extension, that of the child-king, the pharaoh.

Naos - It has two significations: the stone tabernacle in which the statute of the god was placed, and also the enclosed shrine areas that were reserved for statues in ancient Egyptian temples.

Nilometer - The reason why the Egyptians invented the nilometer was their imperative need to monitor the fluctuations of the Nile, particularly during the floods. It was generally installed inside the temple compound and consisted of a long descending stairway leading to the phreatic aquifer. The graduation marks on the walls of the gallery indicating the volume of the water in the river helped to determine the size and the date of the coming flood, particularly at **Elephantine**.

Nome - It is the name given by the Greeks to the administrative regions of the Nile valley. The number, names and territorial limits of the nomes changed incessantly during the thirty centuries of Egypt's history, according to the social and political reforms. But whatever the period, the nome remains an economic and fiscal entity, each one respecting its own temples, gods and laws.

Nubia - This geographical zone stretches from the city of **Khartum**, now the capital of Sudan, to the Egyptian border. During the pharaonic period, **Nubia** was totally dominated by Egypt and used only as a source of gold, wood, stone, cattle and manpower and as a transit zone for the riches from Africa: ivory, ebony, rare animals and essential oils.

Opet (feast of) - This feast was celebrated on the day of the Egyptian new year, in the second month of the flood. Although it was probably observed all over Egypt, our source of information is the detailed accounts of it from the great temple at **Karnak**. The gods of the Theben triad, *Amun*, *Mut* and *Khons*, were brought up the Nile to the temple of **Luxor**, the "Southern Harem," amid cheering crowds who chanted incantations and offered them food and donations. The festivities lasted for about ten days, during which there were not only the ritual celebrations, but also oracles by *Amun* concerning problems and dilemmas that had proved insoluble. At the end of the celebrations, the gods returned to their principal residence at **Karnak** by the same route.

Ostracon - Because of its cost, papyrus was reserved for official or religious use; therefore, private letters or texts, personal notes, rough drafts and outlines were made on less noble materials, such as pottery shards or limestone chips. These documents are called **ostracon**. Some of them are very valuable as they give us quite detailed information of the daily life of the ancient Egyptians—for example, those found at **Deir el-Medina**, the village inhabited by the men working in the **Valley of the Kings** during the New Kingdom.

Psychostasis - This Greek word means "the weighing of the soul," and refers to the Chapter CXXV of the "**Book of the Dead**," when the deceased is introduced by *Anubis* to the judgment hall and his heart is put on a balance tray. *Ma'at*, the symbol of righteousness, is placed in counter balance. This weighing, watched by *Thoth*, is to determine whether the deceased is worthy to enter the realms of *Osiris*. The "Great Eater," a monstruous hybrid being, stays by scales, ready to claim its victims in case of an unfavorable judgment.

Pylon -This element of architecture marks the monumental entrance to a temple. A pylon is composed of two massive trapezoidal piles flanking the gate that gives access to the cult site. Very often, their fronts are decorated with pictues of a pharoah of heroic proportions offering to the god a handful of enemies whom he clutches by their hair.

Pyramid Texts - They are the funerary texts engraved on the walls of the pyramids built up at the end of the Old Kingdom. The oldest text goes back to the time of ***Unas***, the last king of the 5th dynasty. All the kings of the 6th dynasty had them inscribed. But they disappear with the troubles of the First Intermediate Period. Magical spells, different hymns and religious incantations have to secure the king immortality and to allow him to identify himself with the sun.

Royal head-dress - The most common headdress worn by the pharaohs are the following: a simple wig fastened by a head-band and the **nemes**, a striped cloth covering the shoulders; the white crown of Upper Egypt and the red crown of Lower Egypt; the **pschent** combining the two; the **khepresh** or war crown, resembling a helmet, blue with circular dots.

Royal Titulary - They are the five names taken by the pharaoh upon ascending the throne. I: the **Horus name** (I) - II: the **Nebti name** (or **He of the Two Ladies**) - III: the **Golden Horus name** - IV: the **Throne name** (or **He of the Sedge and the Bee**) - V: the **Birth name** (or **Son of Re'**).

Sacred animals - The Egyptians think that any animal is the receptacle of a part of the divine power, whether good or bad. That explains the large number of cults of sacred animals: the crocodile (god *Sobek*), the ibis or the baboon (god *Thoth*), the cat (goddess *Bastet*), the bull (god *Apis*), the falcon (god *Horus*), and the jackal (god *Anubis*) are the main ones.

Sacred lake - All the temple compounds include not only the buildings required for the religious ceremonies but also a pool, rectangular or eccentric in shape, which is reached by several flights of stairs: the sacred lake. The priests purify themselves in its water and the ships carrying their gods navigate on it; on the banks, certain mysteries are celebrated . Its main purpose was, however, to recall the primeval ocean, the *Nun*, from which all life had emerged.

Scepters - These attributes, held by gods, pharaohs and nobles have to determine the qualities and functions of those who carry them. The **heqa** scepter (cross), the **flagellum** (flail) for the god *Osiris* and the pharaoh; the **was** scepter (staff topped by a canine head) for male dieties; the **wadj** scepter (staff in the shape of a papyrus stalk) for female deities; the **sekhem** scepter (a short officer's stick) for the nobles.

Scepters - These attributes, held by gods, kings and noblemen, have to determine the qualities and functions of those who carries them. The most common divine scepters are the following: the **heka** scepter (crook) and the **flail** for the god ***Osiris***, the **wadj** scepter (rod as a stalk of papyrus) for the feminine deities, and the **was** scepter (a long stick with a canine head) for the masculine deities.

Sema-tawi - This Egyptian term is translated as *"to unite the Two Lands."* It is symbolized by two emblematic plants: the lotus of Upper Egypt and the papyrus of Lower Egypt, entwined around a trachea by two deities, *Horus* and *Seth*, or two gods *Ha'py*. This trachea in hieroglyphic writing means "to unite". The **sema-tawi** represents the union between the South and the North in one kingdom.

Serdab - This is the room in the upper story of a **mastaba** which contains the statue of the **ka** of the deceased. It is totally closed-in, and the only communication with the funerary chapel is through a slit in one wall which is meant to allow the statue to enjoy the offerings deposited in the chapel by the deceased's family and friends.

Serekh - A rectangle representing the front of a palace, topped by the symbol of a hawk or falcon, in which the first name of the king was inscribed: the **Name of Horus**.

Theogamy - This term is used for a marriage that unites the Great Royal Wife to the god for the purpose of producing the future sovereign and, in disputed cases, allows a controversial king to accede to the throne.

Uraeus - This word designates the cobra with the extended hood, the eye of *Re'* of the Heliopolitan legend, topping the royal headdress. It is said that he protects the king everywhere and in any event "*even during the night when he sleeps*" and repels all the enemies of Pharaoh.

Ushabti (Shabti or ***Shawabti)*** - Put in the tomb, this mummiform figurine must do all the daily tasks for the deceased in the Underworld. A few words are carved on them: "*O Ushabti! If X (the deceased) is required to do one of the tasks in the next world... You will say: Here I am!*" Appearing during the Middle Kingdom, the **ushabties** are made, according to the deceased's status, of wood, bronze, faience, stone or terra-cotta. Sometimes there are hundreds of them in the same tomb.

Writing - The Egyptians have used three main forms of writing: a sacred writing, the **hieroglyphic**, remarkable for the delicacy of its drawings, and two civil writings, much simpler, the **hieratic** taken over by the **demotic** as far back as the 7th century B.C.

Delta of the Nile, Lower Egypt

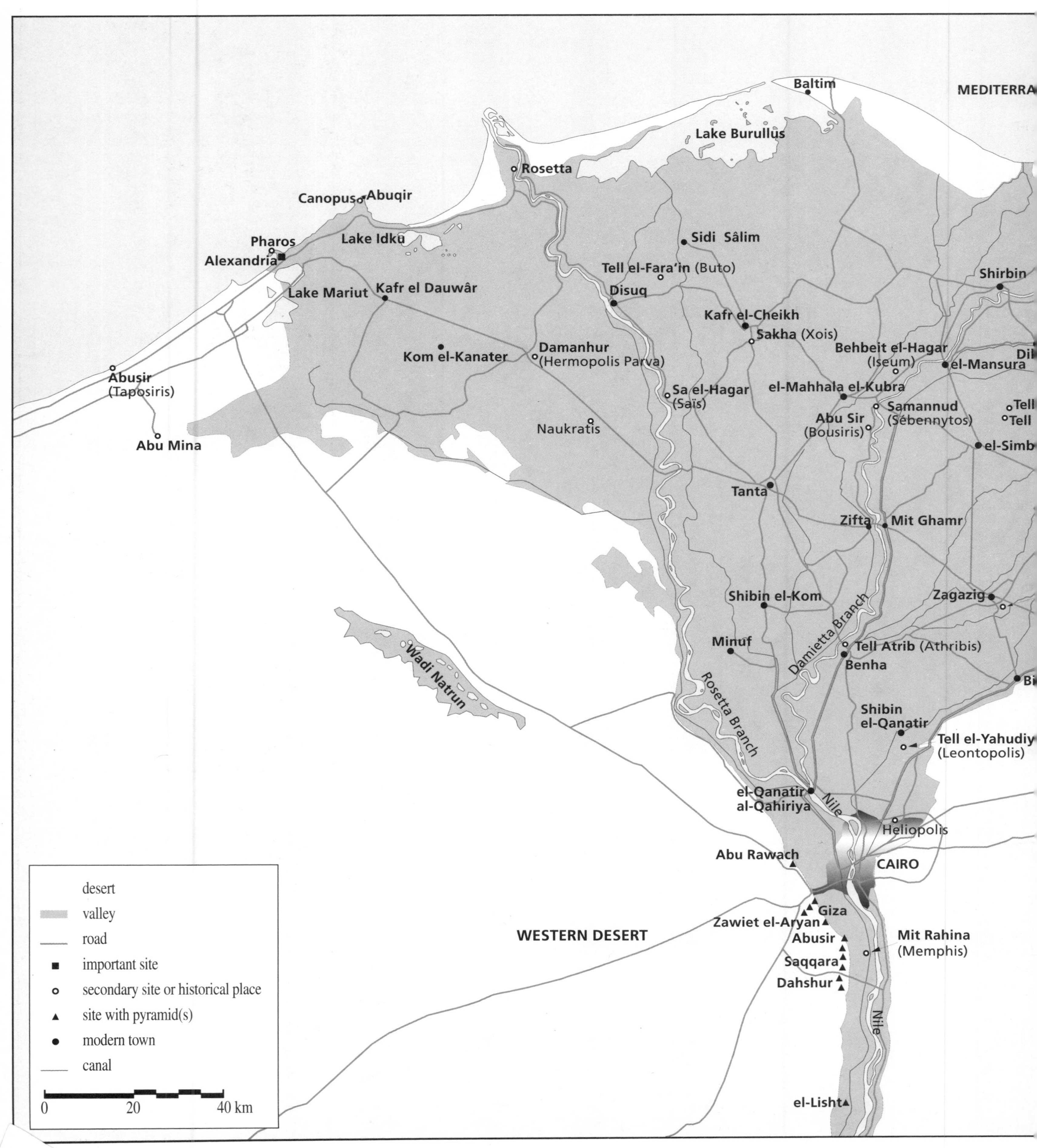

MIDDLE EGYPT

el-Barr
Damietta
Lake Menzala
Port-Said
el-Matariya
el-Menzala
Suez Canal
(Mendes)
(Thmuis)
San el-Hagar
(Tanis)
Tell Dafana
(Daphnae)
el-Qantara
Faqûs
Wadi Tumilat
Ismailia
Tell el-Maskhuta
(Pithom ?)
Great
Bitter
Lake
EASTERN DESERT
To Suez

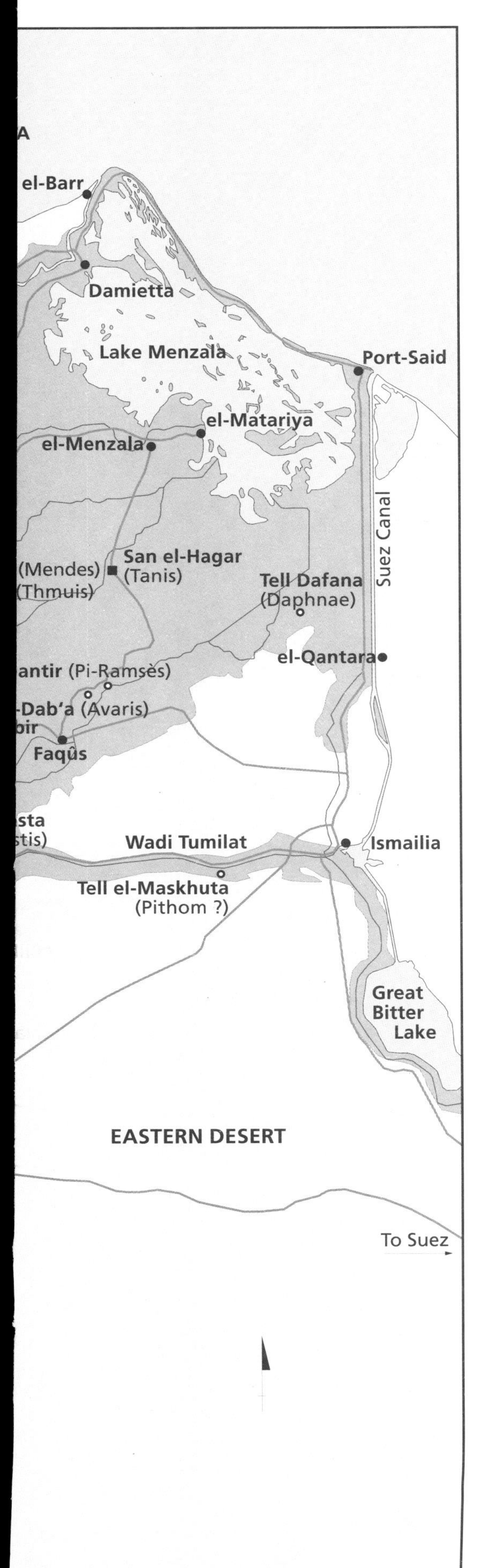

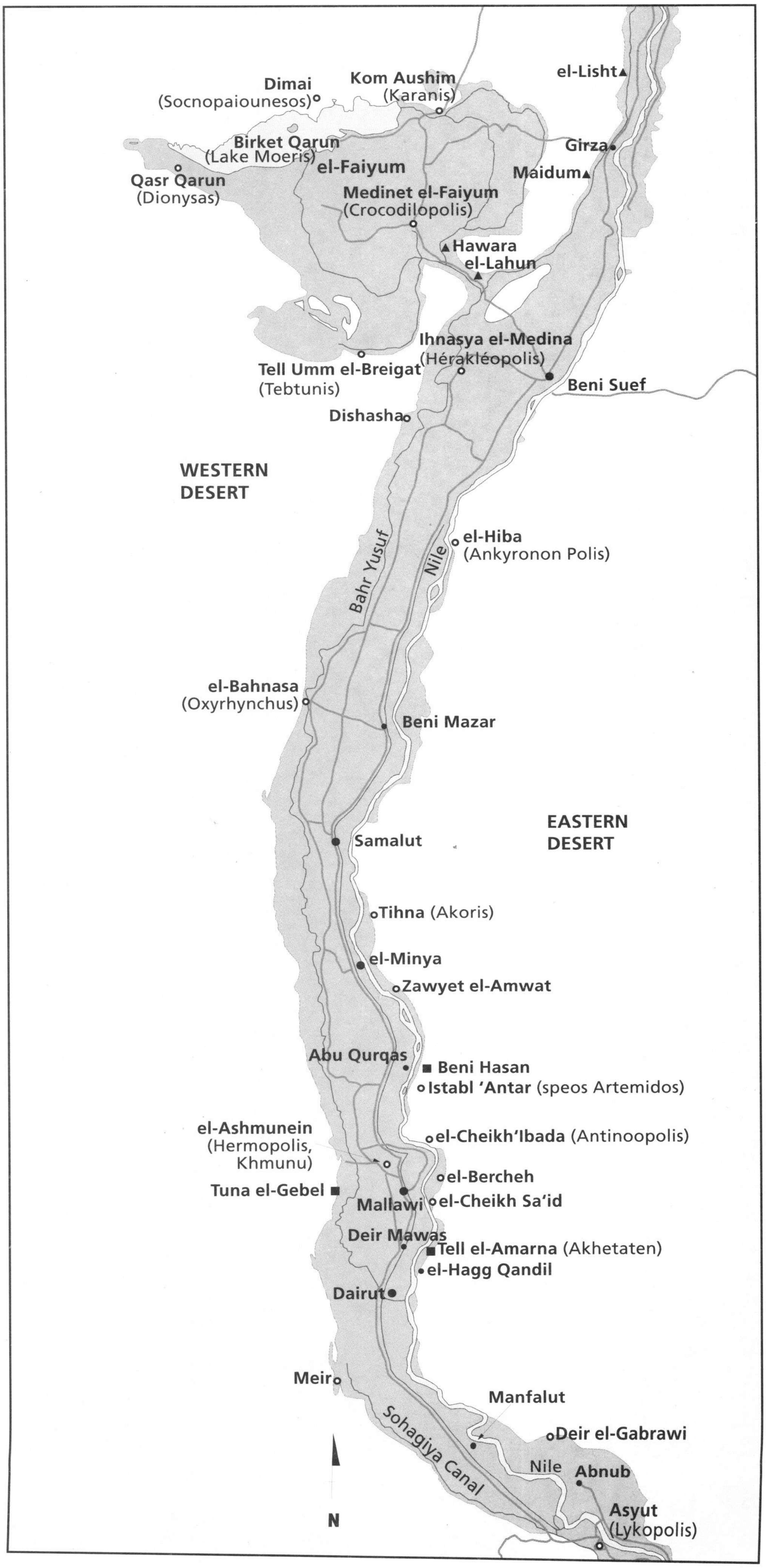

Dimai
(Socnopaiounesos)
Kom Aushim
(Karanis)
el-Lisht
Birket Qarun
(Lake Moeris)
Qasr Qarun
(Dionysas)
el-Faiyum
Girza
Maidum
Medinet el-Faiyum
(Crocodilopolis)
Hawara
el-Lahun
Ihnasya el-Medina
(Hérakléopolis)
Tell Umm el-Breigat
(Tebtunis)
Beni Suef
Dishasha
WESTERN
DESERT
el-Hiba
(Ankyronon Polis)
Bahr Yusuf
Nile
el-Bahnasa
(Oxyrhynchus)
Beni Mazar
Samalut
EASTERN
DESERT
Tihna (Akoris)
el-Minya
Zawyet el-Amwat
Abu Qurqas
Beni Hasan
Istabl 'Antar (speos Artemidos)
el-Ashmunein
(Hermopolis,
Khmunu)
el-Cheikh'Ibada (Antinoopolis)
el-Bercheh
Tuna el-Gebel
Mallawi
el-Cheikh Sa'id
Deir Mawas
Tell el-Amarna (Akhetaten)
el-Hagg Qandil
Dairut
Meir
Manfalut
Sohagiya Canal
Deir el-Gabrawi
Nile
Abnub
Asyut
(Lykopolis)
N

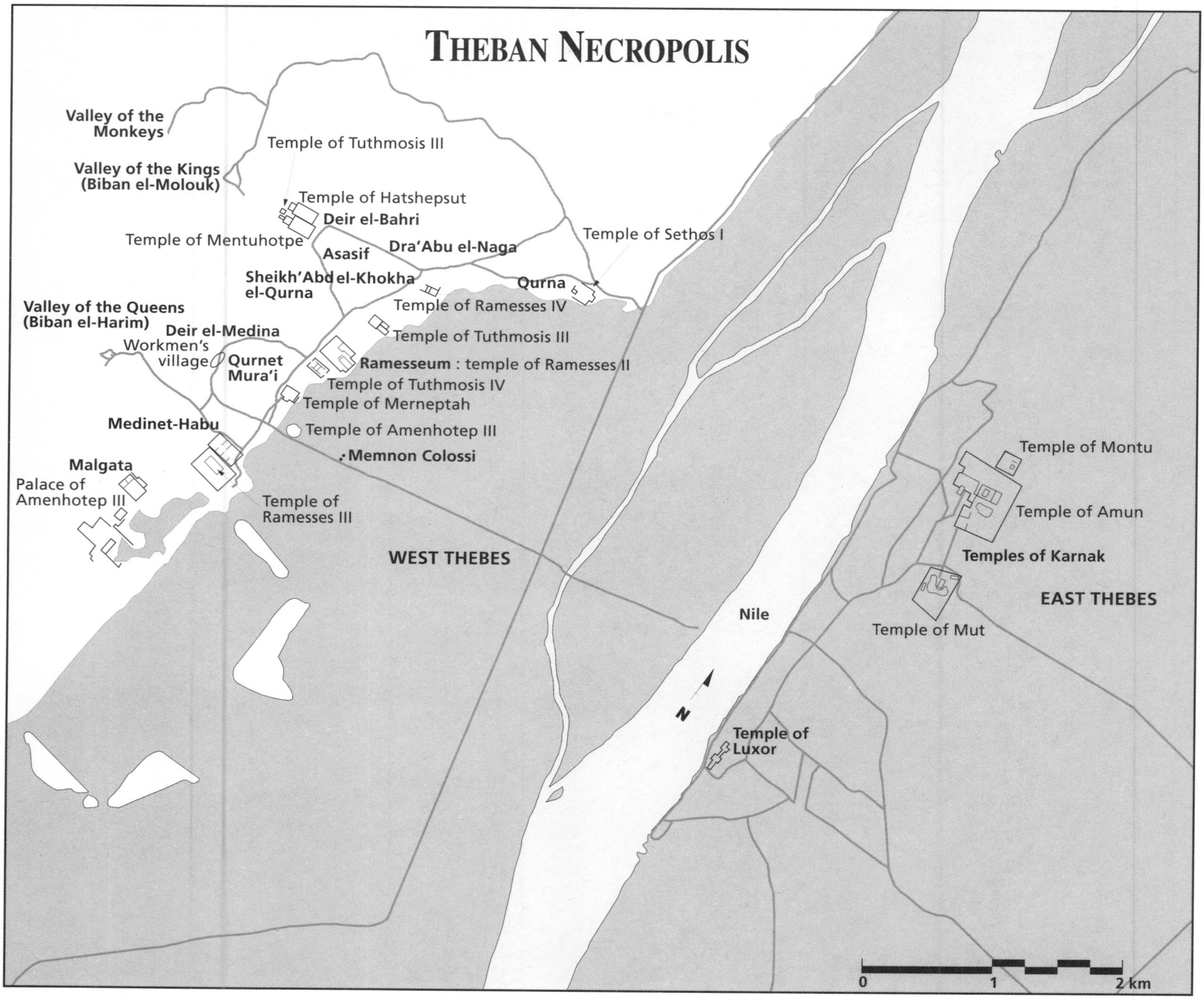

THEBAN NECROPOLIS

Valley of the Monkeys
Temple of Tuthmosis III
Valley of the Kings (Biban el-Molouk)
Temple of Hatshepsut
Deir el-Bahri
Temple of Mentuhotpe
Asasif
Dra'Abu el-Naga
Temple of Sethos I
Sheikh'Abd el-Qurna
el-Khokha
Qurna
Temple of Ramesses IV
Valley of the Queens (Biban el-Harim)
Deir el-Medina
Temple of Tuthmosis III
Workmen's village
Qurnet Mura'i
Ramesseum : temple of Ramesses II
Temple of Tuthmosis IV
Temple of Merneptah
Medinet-Habu
Temple of Amenhotep III
Memnon Colossi
Malgata
Palace of Amenhotep III
Temple of Ramesses III
WEST THEBES
Temple of Montu
Temple of Amun
Temples of Karnak
EAST THEBES
Temple of Mut
Nile
N
Temple of Luxor
0 1 2 km

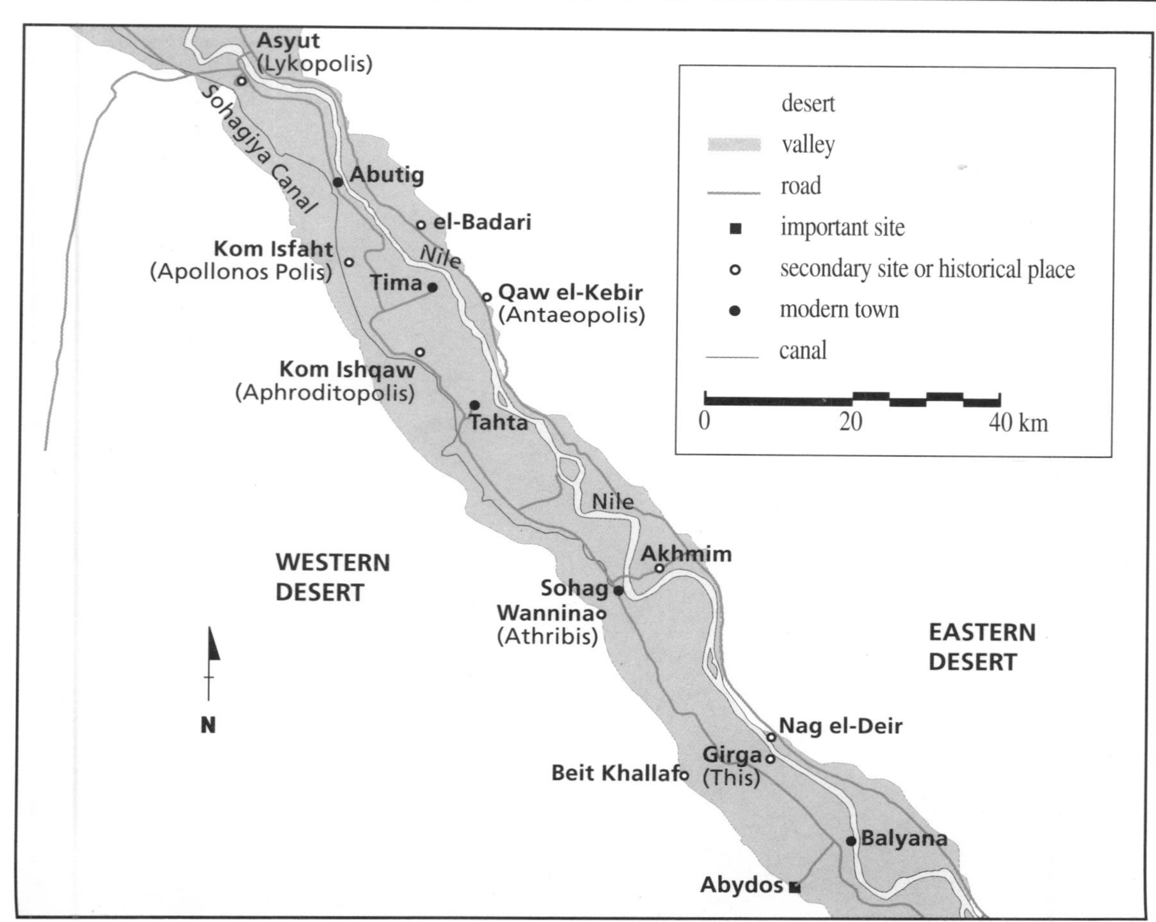

UPPER EGYPT

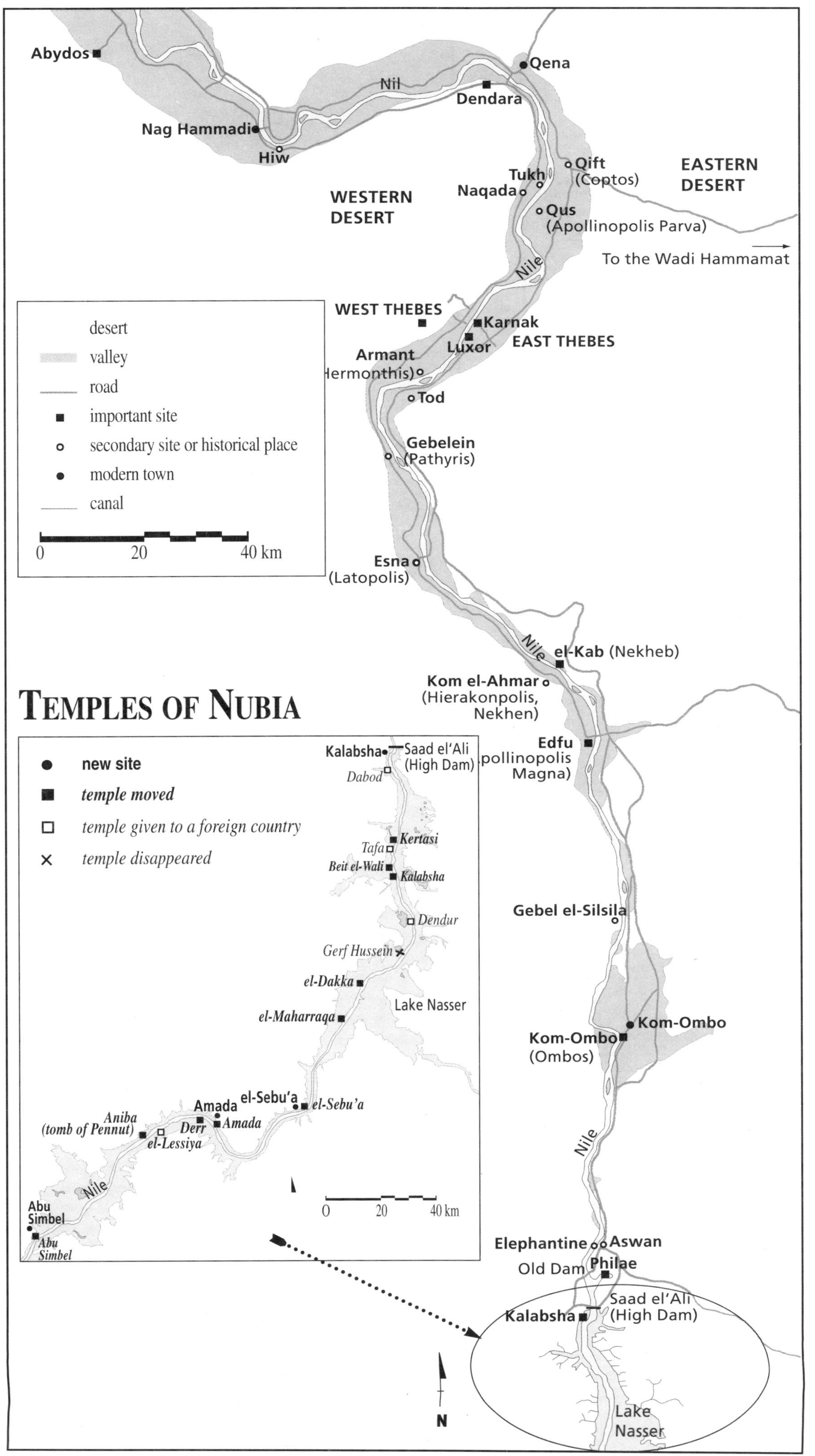

Abydos
Qena
Nil
Dendara
Nag Hammadi
Hiw
Qift
(Coptos)
EASTERN
DESERT
Tukh
Naqada
WESTERN
DESERT
Qus
(Apollinopolis Parva)
To the Wadi Hammamat
Nile
desert
valley
road
important site
secondary site or historical place
modern town
canal
0
20
40 km
WEST THEBES
Karnak
Luxor
EAST THEBES
Armant
(Hermonthis)
Tod
Gebelein
(Pathyris)
Esna
(Latopolis)
Nile
el-Kab (Nekheb)
Kom el-Ahmar
(Hierakonpolis,
Nekhen)
TEMPLES OF NUBIA
new site
temple moved
temple given to a foreign country
temple disappeared
Kalabsha
Saad el'Ali
(High Dam)
Dabod
Kertasi
Tafa
Beit el-Wali
Kalabsha
Dendur
Gerf Hussein
el-Dakka
Lake Nasser
el-Maharraqa
el-Sebu'a
el-Sebu'a
Amada
Amada
Derr
Aniba
(tomb of Pennut)
el-Lessiya
Nile
Abu
Simbel
Abu
Simbel
0
20
40 km
Edfu
(Apollinopolis
Magna)
Gebel el-Silsila
Kom-Ombo
Kom-Ombo
(Ombos)
Nile
Elephantine
Aswan
Old Dam
Philae
Saad el'Ali
(High Dam)
Kalabsha
Lake
Nasser
N

THE VALLEY OF THE NILE

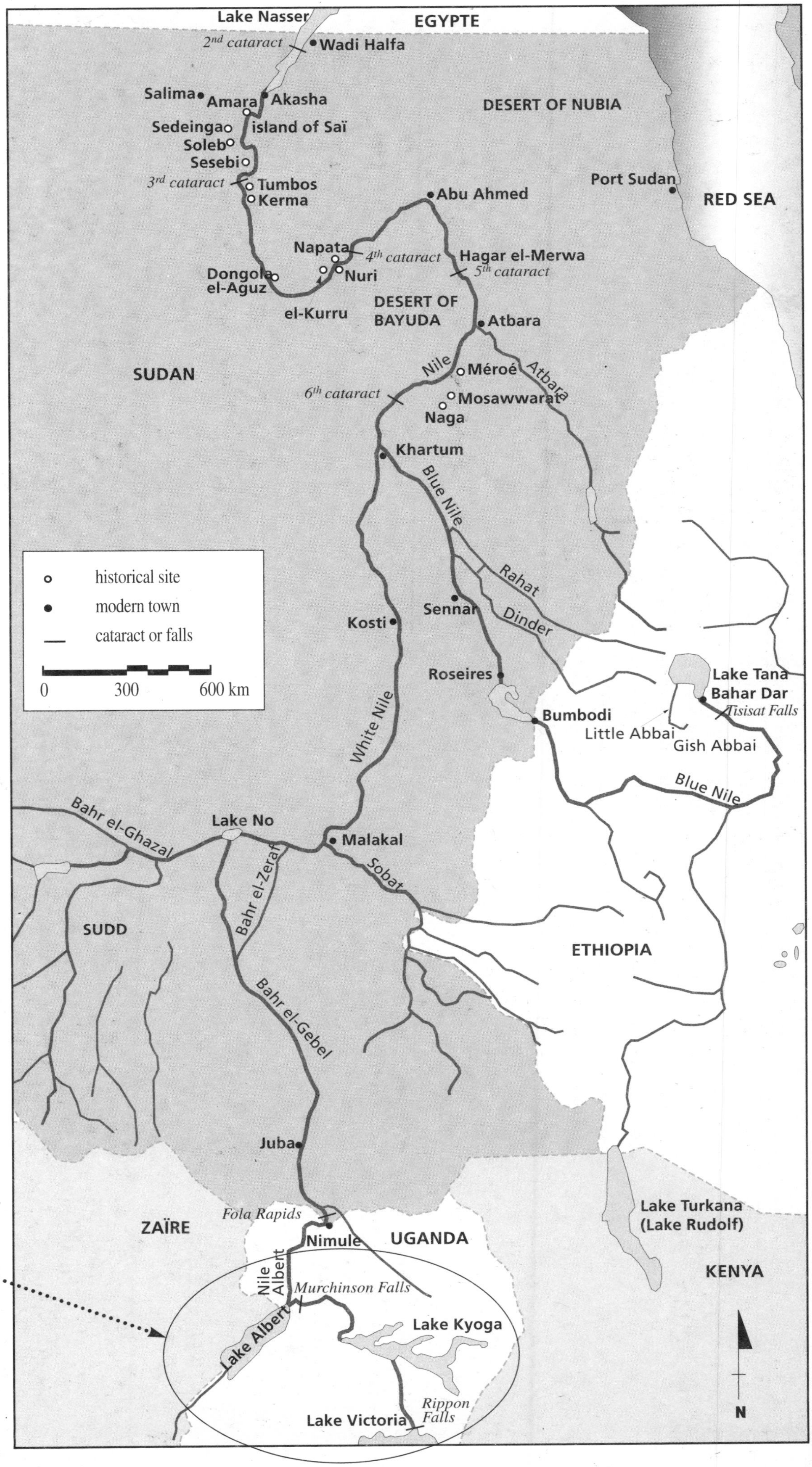

Lake Nasser
EGYPTE
2nd cataract
Wadi Halfa
Salima
Amara
Akasha
DESERT OF NUBIA
Sedeinga
island of Saï
Soleb
Sesebi
3rd cataract
Tumbos
Kerma
Port Sudan
RED SEA
Abu Ahmed
Napata
4th cataract
Hagar el-Merwa
5th cataract
Nuri
Dongola el-Aguz
el-Kurru
DESERT OF BAYUDA
Atbara
SUDAN
Nile
Méroé
Atbara
6th cataract
Mosawwarat
Naga
Khartum
Blue Nile
historical site
modern town
cataract or falls
0
300
600 km
Rahat
Kosti
Sennar
Dinder
Roseires
Lake Tana
Bahar Dar
Tisisat Falls
Bumbodi
Little Abbai
Gish Abbai
White Nile
Blue Nile
Bahr el-Ghazal
Lake No
Malakal
Bahr el-Zeraf
Sobat
SUDD
ETHIOPIA
Bahr el-Gebel
Juba
Fola Rapids
ZAÏRE
Nimule
UGANDA
Lake Turkana (Lake Rudolf)
KENYA
Nile Albert
Murchinson Falls
Lake Albert
Lake Kyoga
Rippon Falls
Lake Victoria
N

SOURCES OF THE NILE

Nile
Lake Albert
Murchinson Falls
Lake Kyoga
Ruwenzori
Rippon Falls
Lake Edouard
Lake Victoria (Lake Nyanza)
Lake Kivu
Muanza
Lualaba
Lake Tanganyika
Zanzibar
Lake Bangouelo
Lake Nyassa
Chitambo
Mozambique
0
200
400 km

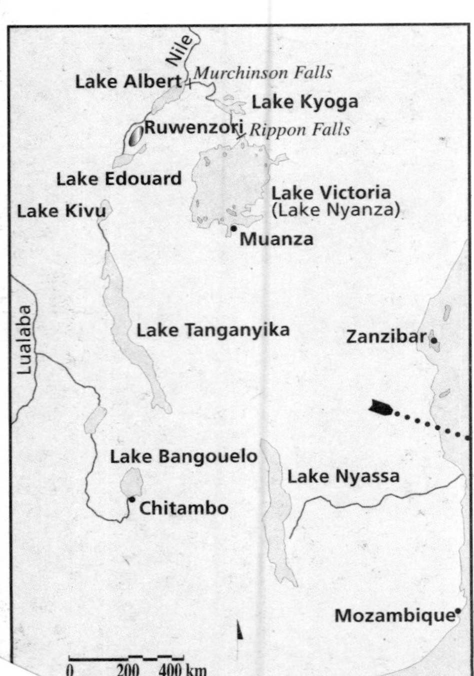

BIBLIOGRAPHY

Cyril Aldred,
The Egyptians, Thames and Hudson, London / New York, 1961 / 1984

John Baines et Jaromir Malek,
Atlas of Ancient Egypt, Andromeda, Oxford, 1980 and 1996

Paul Barguet,
Le Livre des Morts des Anciens Égyptiens - Les Textes des Sarcophages des Égyptiens du Moyen Empire (two volumes),
Cerf, Littérature Ancienne du Proche Orient (LAPO), 1967 and 1986

Maria Carmela Betró,
Hiéroglyphes, les mystères de l'écriture, Flammarion, 1995

Peter A. Clayton,
Chronicle of the Pharaohs,
Thames and Hudson, London, 1994 and 1999

Marc Collier and Bill Manley,
How to read Egyptian hieroglyphs,
British Museum Press, London, 1998 and 1999

Christiane Desroches-Noblecourt,
Toutankhamon, vie et mort d'un pharaon, Pygmalion, 1988

Christiane Desroches-Noblecourt,
Amours et fureur de la Lointaine, Stock, Paris, 1995

Mircea Eliade,
Traité d'histoire des religions, Payot, Paris, 1987

Raymond O. Faulkner,
The Ancient Egyptian Book of the Dead,
under the management of C. Andrews, London, 1985 and 1996

Raymond O. Faulkner,
The Ancient Egyptian Pyramid Texts (two volumes), Oxford, 1969

Henri Frankfort,
Ancient Egyptian Religion, New York, 1948

Sir Allan Gardiner,
Egypt of the Pharaohs, Oxford / New York, 1961

John Gwyn Griffiths,
The conflict of Horus and Seth from Egyptian and Classical sources,
Liverpool, 1960

John Gwyn Griffiths,
Plutarch's De Iside et Osiride, Swansea, 1970

Nicolas Grimal,
Histoire de l'Égypte ancienne, Fayard, 1988

George Hart,
Egyptian myths, British Museum Press

Herodotus,
Histories, Book II, A. B. Lloyd,
Herodotus Book II.1: an intoduction (Leiden, 1975)
Herodotus Book II.2: commentary 1-98 (Leiden, 1976)
Herodotus Book II.2: commentary 99-182 (Leiden, 1988)

Erik Hornung,
Der Eine und die Vielen, Darmstadt, 1971

Claire Lalouette,
Textes sacrés et textes profanes de l'Ancienne Égypte,
Connaissances de l'Orient, Gallimard UNESCO, Paris, 1984

Claire Lalouette,
Au royaume d'Égypte - Thèbes ou la naissance d'un empire - L'empire des Ramsès (three volumes),
New edition, Collection Champs, Flammarion, 1995

Mark Lehner,
The complete Pyramids, Thames and Hudson, London

Dimitri Meeks et Christine Favard-Meeks,
La vie quotidienne des dieux égyptiens, Hachette, 1993

Siegfried Morenz,
Osiris und Amun, Kult und Heilige Stätten, Munich, 1966

Georges Posener, Serge Sauneron et Jean Yoyotte,
Dictionnaire de la civilisation égyptienne, Hazan, 1959

Donald B. Redford,
Akhénaton, the heretic king, Princeton, 1995

Nicholas Reeves,
The complete Tutankhamun, Thames and Hudson, London, 1990

Nicholas Reeves and Richard H. Wilkinson,
The complete Valley of the Kings, Thames and Hudson, London

Serge Sauneron et Jean Yoyotte,
La naissance du monde selon l'Égypte ancienne,
Sources Orientales I, Seuil, Paris, 1959

Ian Shaw et Paul Nicholson,
British Museum, Dictionary of Ancient Egypt,
British Museum Press, 1995

Jacques Vandier,
Manuel d'archéologie égyptienne (six volumes de texte et deux volumes de planches), Éditions A. et J. Picard & Cie, Paris, 1952 à 1964

Jacques Vandier,
La religion égyptienne, Paris, P.U.F., Collection "Mana", 1949